BORN
FOR
LOVE

Reflections on Loving

Other books by Leo Buscaglia

Love

Living, Loving & Learning

Personhood

Because I Am Human

The Way of the Bull

The Disabled and Their Parents:
A Counseling Challenge

Loving Each Other

Bus 9 to Paradise

The Fall of Freddie the Leaf

A Memory for Tino

Seven Stories of Christmas Love

Papa, My Father

BORN
FOR
LOVE

Reflections on Loving

by
Leo F. Buscaglia, Ph.D.

Edited by Daniel Kimber

Published by SLACK Incorporated
Distributed by Random House, Inc.

FOR STEVEN SHORT
WITH GRATITUDE, ADMIRATION AND LOVE.

Printed in the United States of America

Random House, Inc. ISBN: 0-679-41393-6

There are several sources for the many quotations on
these pages. Credit is given where possible.
I am deeply indebted to their authors.

I also want to express gratitude to Daniel Kimber,
my editor; Debbie Anderson, Peter Slack,
Barbara and Charles Slack and Carol Spain.

WE ARE ALL BORN FOR LOVE.
IT IS THE PRINCIPLE OF EXISTENCE,
AND ITS ONLY END
Benjamin Disraeli

Table of Contents

Introduction

I begin each day by listening to the news. I hear of the jogger who got mugged in the park, the child wounded by a madman's bullet, the husband who strangled his wife in a jealous rage, another municipal scandal, new racial killings, complaints of our bogged-down judicial system, and over-crowded prisons erupting in violence. In spite of this, I eat my breakfast, get dressed, and with renewed determination, secure in my armor of optimism, I face the world as a lover. I know that this may seem naive and perhaps a little simplistic to the cynic, but as far as I can determine, it is the only sensible decision.

It is difficult for some people to accept that love is a choice. This seems to run counter to the generally accepted theory of romantic love which expounds that love is inborn and as such requires no more than to accept it. This theory believes that love is a magical force which frees us from all suffering and solves every problem, that it is an end unto itself. To a limited extent, there may be some truth to each of these beliefs, but having the capacity to love is not the same as having the ability to love.

Love is certainly genetically inscribed, but it needs to be evoked, studied, taught and practiced if it is to have any real meaning.

To date, even our keenest minds and most sophisticated technology have been unsuccessful in unraveling the ways, powers and mysteries of love. So, any talk of love continues to elicit churning intellectual and emotional responses. It is dismissed by some as a disease of self-delusion, an affront to common sense, and an impediment to self control. At the same time, others celebrate it as the greatest of human values, a direct gift from God, the most powerful and potent life enhancing human energy, and possibly life's only meaning.

Having dedicated myself to the study of love for the past

two and a half decades, you may be sure that I have often been accused of being an incurable, hopeless romantic. I don't deny it. But as far as I can tell, this is an advantage, not a detriment. I may be unsophisticated and gullible, but love has shown the way for a most exciting, full and wonderful life. I am still leading with my heart. I have certainly had it messed with from time to time, but I find that the heart heals and one can function very well with a bruised heart.

But I am not so naive as to believe that one can succeed as a lover guided solely by a heart beat. We also possess a mind. Love can benefit from serious study, analysis and learning.

Choosing to be a lover doesn't preclude common sense, nor does it mean that we check our brains at the door. Those whose love relationships are nothing but emotional roller coasters may find that their intellects provide a stabilizing influence for a smoother ride.

It is an injustice to speak of "love at first sight," "happy every aftering" and "unconditional loving," as if they were givens, to be expected simply because we are human. We continue to resist any notion that love is learned, that it takes great conscious effort to acquire the requisite skills to keep love alive. Rather, the majority of us are prone to wait until we find ourselves despairing, lonely, and overpowered by feelings of hopelessness before we look to a better understanding of love as a possible answer. So we continue to scoff at love. And the result? More loneliness, more aspirins, more high blood pressure, more psychotherapists, more ulcers, more antacids, more breakdowns, more heart attacks, more headaches, more frigidity, more impotence, more insomnia, more laxatives, more anorexia, more overeating, more weariness, more boredom, more despair, more suspicion, more drugs, more intoxication, more mistakes, more frustration, more fear, more suicides, more hate, more prejudice, more killing, more prisons, more divorces, more failures, more sadness, more envy, more pain, more violence, more ignorance, more bigotry, more stupidity, more apathy, more tears, more death.

It is my wish that this book can help us out of this dilemma. It offers some thoughts which I hope will elicit serious analysis, stimulate feelings and eventually lead to actions which encourage change and growth. I have tried to state these ideas simply and (hopefully) clearly, repeating some of them for emphasis.

This book is not intended as a "how to." It is more of a "how about?" It has no real beginning or end and can be picked up at any point. It is the reader who becomes a personal guide.

Though there are innumerable thoughts offered here, they are actually all part of a single concept. Love is not some complex, mystical abstraction. It is something accessible and human that we learn through our everyday experience, as often at times of failure as in moments of ecstasy.

This book is for students of love, for men and women who are eager to search for the best that life has to offer and who are determined not to die before they have discovered, developed and released their potential for love.

Reflections on loving.

Love requires effort

Love never dies a natural death. It dies from neglect and abandonment. It dies of blindness and indifference and of being taken for granted. Things omitted are often more deadly than errors committed.

In the end, love dies of weariness, from not being nurtured. We don't really fall out of love any more than we fall into it. When love dies, one or both partners have neglected it, have failed to replenish and renew it. Like any other living, growing thing, love requires effort to keep it healthy.

The great tragedy of life is not that men perish,
but that they cease to love.
W. SOMERSET MAUGHAM

Failure in love

There is no failure where love is concerned. To be unsuccessful is not the same as failure. Our disappointment is more likely to provide an opportunity to learn and to grow.

If we don't risk loving, we will never fail in love. But much worse, we will also never experience its wonder. As Lloyd Jones assures us, those who try to do something and fail are infinitely better off than those who try to do nothing and succeed.

We seem to gain wisdom more readily through our failures than through our successes. We always think of failure as the antithesis of success, but it isn't. Success often lies just the other side of failure.

As long as we continue to seek love, some failure is bound to occur. But hurt is a strong impetus for action. When we seek to find the causes of our failures, we always emerge wiser. We gain new alternatives for our old behaviors and acquire new resources for future encounters. This is certainly not failure. Rather, it is the way that produces lasting change. It is the way of insight and growth. It is the way of love.

There is no failure except in no longer trying.
ELBERT HUBBARD

We come into this world ignorant of love—some of us leave the same way

Our world remains a mystery, even to the most knowledgeable among us. We often look toward professionals, political leaders or celebrities for the answers to our problems with life and love, only to be disillusioned by their feet of clay. If we are wise, we discover that our answers come only when we work them out for ourselves. Others may contribute to our understanding, but the acquiring of personal wisdom is always an inside job. No one can do it for us.

Additionally, knowledge often comes by way of ignorance, so we should all be challenged and encouraged by what we don't know.

I've studied love for the better part of my life and am amazed at how much there still is to learn.

Too many of us are born ignorant of love and are content to remain so. There is nothing wrong with making mistakes and not having all the answers, so long as we are willing to admit this and strive for personal betterment. Those who think they know it all have no way of finding out that they don't.

Every time you acquire a new interest, even more, a new accomplishment, you increase your power of life.
WILLIAM LYON PHELPS

Rigidity and loving

I had a great Buddhist teacher many years ago in Thailand who taught emotional survival with a simple illustration. "Be like the bamboo," he'd say. "It is strong on the outside, soft and open on the inside. Its roots are firmly planted in the ground and freely intertwined with others for mutual strength and support. The stalk blows freely in the wind, bending rather than resisting. That which bends is far more difficult to break."

We sometimes handle frustration and pressure better by yielding to it than attempting to stand firm against it each time it occurs. Things are not usually all good or all bad, all right or all wrong. Life is just not that simple. The answers and solutions we seek usually lie somewhere between the opposites. When we insist on seeing things as only black or white, we are further removed from understanding; further isolated from truth. Giving in does not imply giving up any more than being flexible is a sign of lacking conviction. Most often, by being willing to give a little, we get more than we ever dreamed.

With so many spectacular colors in the world, it's a shame to make
everything black and white.
DENNIS R. LITTLE

The agelessness of love

I was walking through a park once with a friend. Though we saw many young lovers as we strolled on our way, my friend made no comment until he encountered two elderly people being rather amorous on one of the park benches. "That's weird," he commented. "They're a little old for that, don't you think?"

I find it interesting—and, as I grow older, rather appalling—that we relegate romance only to the young. This comes from the false notion that passions cool as we age. Vitality and attractiveness are lost, along with the appetite for love and romance.

This is nonsense! Love lasts as long as we draw a breath. In reality, our options may have grown, reflecting the accumulation of a lifetime of wisdom. Feelings may have deepened and become even more velvety and rich with time.

Living in love, no matter our age, simply means we have learned to keep our love vital. Aged love, like aged wine, becomes more satisfying, more refreshing, more valuable, more appreciated, more intoxicating. Experienced lovers need only smile in forgiveness at the very young for their incomplete understanding of love, and drink fully.

The great thing about getting older is that you don't lose all the other ages you've been.
MADELINE L'ENGLE

Love as a work of art

There are all kinds of artists. A group we should celebrate more are artists of life itself who use their tools to express the inexpressible. Without a brush, they depict life with bright colors. Without a knife, they sculpt the magic of being. Without a scale, they create music for us all. Without choreography, they engage in the dance of life.

When we are born, we are each given tools to create a life of beauty. These same tools can be used to perpetuate ugliness and destruction. Hopefully we will understand at some point in our lives that we can decide to reflect beauty. Tangible works of art fade with time, chip from walls, and may be discredited by passing trends. But a life of love lasts forever.

Nobody has ever measured, even poets,
how much the heart can hold.
ZELDA FITZGERALD

In love, we may
find it better to make
allowances, rather
than make points.

Love and self-respect

People need the proper atmosphere in which to grow and discover their distinctiveness. We are indeed fortunate if someone has taken the time to look closely enough to see our unique spark and help us develop our special abilities.

I read a story once of the very accomplished members of the Taft family. They were apparently very good at recognizing abilities and specialities in family members. When Martha Taft was in elementary school in Cincinnati, she was asked to introduce herself. She said, "My name is Martha Bowers Taft. My great-grandfather was President of the United States. My grandfather was a United States Senator. My daddy is Ambassador to Ireland. And I am a Brownie."

Even when no one else seems to recognize how truly remarkable we are, we always have ourselves, the one inexhaustible resource for positive reinforcement, the one person who will always proudly wave our personal flag.

I am more important than my problems.
JOSE FERRER

Don't wait for love to come to you

Someone once wrote that there is no use waiting for your love boat to come in unless you've sent it out. I am aware that there are many among us who are determined to wait for love, the "someday my prince(ss) will come" belief. For a few fortunate ones, this might be true, but some of us will wait forever, often until we become cynical, embittered human beings, too afraid to love and perhaps even unable to recognize it when it does come.

When I was teaching Love Class, we were once visited by a dog. The dog entered the class fearlessly, wagging its tail and wandering among the seated students, getting all the attention he wanted. The students, of course, responded with pats and caresses, prompting one of the young ladies in the class to observe dryly, "This is so typical of my life. Here I've been hurting all evening with loneliness and not a person has offered me an understanding touch. A stray dog wanders in and is showered with affection! There's something very wrong with that."

"Maybe it's not so crazy," a young man responded. "The dog came in and by his actions told us he was open to loving. His message was simple, nonthreatening and clear. You, on the other hand, just sat there stoically, revealing nothing. We're not mind readers. Sometimes you've just got to speak up, or at least give some hints."

If we want a love message to be heard, it has got to be sent out.
To keep a lamp burning, we have to keep putting oil in it.
MOTHER TERESA

Fear of vulnerability

Some people are convinced they are emotionally safe only when they remain guarded, unexposed and thick-skinned. They are cautious not to truly reveal themselves for fear that in being seen for who they are, they'll be exposed and ultimately left defenseless. Protected and unassailable, their relationships never go beyond a superficial level. At the same time, they lament the absence of the deep intimacy necessary for love.

When we defend, protect and guard, we isolate ourselves into loneliness. We may escape severe emotional trauma, but in so doing, we miss the ultimate joys of true intimacy. Only by allowing ourselves to be vulnerable do we stand a chance of succeeding in love.

If, in the end, we are deceived, betrayed or tricked, we can at least say that we have tried. And, in a sense, we have succeeded if we do not allow the scars of experience to cause us to develop a thick impenetrable skin. When we gain the insight to realize that vulnerability is the soul of love, we will surely heal and try again.

The only true happiness comes
from squandering ourselves for a purpose.
WILLIAM COOPER

Love is nourished by optimism

Those of us who begin a relationship with the fear that it will fail or bring us pain are likely to find ourselves prophets. There is no greater harbinger of failure than to invite it as a possibility. On the other hand, there is every reason to believe that our love will succeed and flourish, that our union with another will bring us even greater possibilities for joy and happiness.

Why shouldn't our future be one of brightness, goodness, productivity and growth? We must live in the hope that every decision we make, every action we perform, will take us in the right direction; in the direction necessary for success in love. Even our mistakes can be cause for optimism by offering us opportunities for new learning and greater awareness.

Love doesn't insist upon perfection, and neither should we. Love thrives in a positive view of self, life and our world. When we keep our focus upon constructive images that enrich relationships, we are less limited by our past and more encouraged by the present. Experience shows that we tend to actualize dreams if we truly want them to happen. Lovers learn not to just hope for the better, they strive to make it happen.

An optimist may see a light where there is none,
but why must the pessimist always run to blow it out?
MICHEL DE SAINT-PIERRE

Love knows what is essential

Some people fear that when beauty fades, so does love. These individuals have little real knowledge of love and less respect for themselves, for in reality, it is the other way around; beauty fades only when love is gone.

Love makes us more comfortable with and accepting of each other's imperfections. Love isn't appalled when we stand in the bathroom in sagging underwear loudly gargling with our hair pointing in all directions. It doesn't care that we've acquired a new set of wrinkles on our face, that our skin is flabbier than it used to be, that we have developed a more substantial midriff. When we love, we see through such inconsequential things. We concentrate on internal beauty that is unaffected by time or age. It is not that love is blind, it is, rather, that love sees what is essential.

*There is no beautifier of complexion, or form, or behavior, like the
wish to scatter joy and not pain around us.*
RALPH WALDO EMERSON

Bringing surprise to love

Even the most ardent lovers tend to be placated and lulled by love. Comfortable, without a ripple of discontent, we take our relationships for granted, and a great complacency descends. This can be a precarious time for love. Symptoms of a developing problem can include a dull acceptance of everything, the desire to remain safe by traveling only familiar paths, and an undefinable feeling that something is missing. The cure involves a willingness to step a little more boldly into paths that excite and astound and renew.

Nothing is so fatal as predictability. Dull routines have a way of insidiously creeping into our lives: Sunday morning breakfast after church at the same restaurant; Wednesdays with the in-laws; Fridays at the movies. This thread of habit is woven into our lives until we find ourselves bound, limited only to experiencing the same small slices of life over and over again. What is so desperately needed in such situations is a serendipitous act, a surprise dinner, an unexpected gift, a little craziness to shake up this deadly, habitual existence.

Love withers with predictability; its very essence is surprise and amazement. To make love a prisoner of the mundane is to take away its passion and lose it forever.

Miracles are instantaneous, they cannot be summoned,
but they come of themselves, usually at the unlikely moments and
to those who least expect them.
KATHERINE ANN PORTER

When love is postponed for another day

The idea of expressing love is treated by many like the book we have been meaning to read or the phone call we intend to make or the letter we plan to write. Our will is genuine, our intentions are good, but there are always good reasons why we do not accomplish it. Perhaps the time is not quite right, the mood is wrong, there are too many more important things to do, the planets are not in proper alignment, any excuse will do! So our days fill with lost opportunities and postponements instead of much needed love.

Some things just shouldn't be put off. A child who comes running to us for a hug or lavish exclamations of praise needs it now, not at our convenience. A friend who requires a shoulder to cry on can't wait for a more opportune time. A lover who needs reassurance shouldn't be put off for any reason. Love is a commitment that assures we will be there when we are needed. The feeling that there might be a more convenient time to love has caused many people a lifetime of regret. There can be no atonement for moments when our love was necessary and we left them unfulfilled.

One who lets slip by the opportunity to serve another
misses one of the richest experiences life has to offer.
PALI TEXT

Love creates an
"us" without
destroying a "me."

A *healthy condition for unconditional love*

We are always hearing about unconditional love. It has become popular to assure lovers that we love them "without conditions," but we soon find it difficult to meet the condition of loving unconditionally. In fact, there is at least one must-be condition to our loving someone, and that is that they continue to grow as an individual, separately from us. If we feel, for an instant, that we are keeping someone from growth, we must, immediately and carefully, examine our love. We must not only respect the need for our lover's growth, we must encourage it, even at the risk of losing them. It seems ironic, but it is true, that only in continuing to grow separately is there any hope of individuals growing together.

It is a fallacy that to maintain love two people must merge completely into one. Tending the hearth together makes a cozy picture until we run out of fuel because neither partner ventures out occasionally to replenish it. When we do, we return to a hearth that burns brighter, and provides more warmth for both of us.

Things do not change, we do.
HENRY DAVID THOREAU

*L*ove as fulfillment

Though there can be no more fulfilling goal in life than to love and be loved, we seldom find these high on people's wish lists. Money, fame, and possessions are generally more desired, because we wrongly assume that if we succeed in these ways, love will flow from them. Nothing can be further from the truth. Sadly, our desires do not often coincide with what is best for us. The material enticements and temporary pleasures of this world are undeniably attractive, but we would be wise to seek more substantial promises of happiness and fulfillment.

When we are fulfilled in love, we can begin to feel a real sense of security, peace and contentment; one that does not fluctuate with the trends of the moment. A loving relationship gives us an inner wealth that outlives the greatest of external pleasures.

People want riches. They need fulfillment.
BOB CONKLIN

The natural flow of love

My mother, on her death bed, chastised me for crying. "What are you holding on to?" she asked. At that moment I was too shocked and saddened to allow the wisdom of her words to settle in my mind. Later, though, I came to understand that she was telling me to get on with life. Her time had passed while most of mine still lay ahead.

I've let go of many things since then and it has made all the difference. I recently moved from a home in which I had lived for over forty years. Memories of joy, pain, beauty, dreams, people and adventures filled every closet and every drawer of every room. I thought I would never be able to abandon this home to strangers.

But, recalling Mama's question, I simply closed the door and left. It was so simple. I realized that the memories and dreams I valued were not hanging in the closets or hiding in the drawers; they were in me and I would be taking them wherever I went.

It's very human to cling to what we have, but in so doing, we destroy the natural ebb and flow of life.

There is a natural movement to loving, as well. It does not begin and end anymore than it remains fixed at one point in our lives. It is continuous and ever expanding, finding abundant expression in new experiences, while living forever in warm memories.

My interest is in the future, because I am going to spend
the rest of my life there.
CHARLES F. KETTERING

24

Love doesn't keep score

Sharing in love does not mean keeping a balance sheet of who is doing what and who is doing more. There will be times when we must give more than we get, but there will be other moments when we will need and receive more than we are able to give. Keeping score belongs in competitive sports, not in a mutually supportive relationship. True love is wanting to give to another person without any thought about who's getting the better of the deal. The idea that love involves some sort of *quid pro quo* is, at best, an immaturity that needs to be outgrown. At worst, it is a distortion of love that turns two people into unhappy combatants vying for control.

Of all the games that lovers play, this can be one of the most delicate. When the players are mature enough and care enough to stop keeping score, the contest is over. Love has declared another victory.

There are many truths of which the full meaning cannot be
realized until personal experience has brought it home.
JOHN STUART MILL

The search for love

Nothing, except perhaps the Fountain of Youth, has ever led us on a more constant or frantic search than love. We begin the search as children and it never ends until the day we die.

I'm convinced that we cannot live without love. The problem is that love is so changing, so elusive, has so many faces, that one who pursues it often falls into frustration. Perhaps it would be better to stop pursuing and just live it.

Love may come to those of us who wait, but it had better be an *active* waiting, not a passive one, or we may wait forever.

If you would be loved, love and be lovable.
BENJAMIN FRANKLIN

Love has nothing to do with competition

It's unfortunate that so many of us are encouraged to develop a competitive spirit early in life because it so often works to the detriment of a cooperative spirit necessary for love. The world becomes an arena of winners and losers, where character is shaped according to one's ability to survive, where winning is the only sign of success and where we are constantly measured against others to determine and validate our worth.

Love is not a competitive sport. Winning in love comes through cooperation, compromise and caring. When we become masters of these skills, everybody wins.

We cannot live only for ourselves. A thousand fibers connect us
with our fellow men; and along these fibers, as sympathetic
threads, our actions run as causes, and they come back as effects.
HERMAN MELVILLE

One who relaxes in
the arms of love
usually awakens at
the feet of
disillusionment.

*N*ever tire of saying *"I love you"*

Such a simple phrase, "I love you," yet I cannot think of any words with greater power. Francois Villon, the French poet, wrote, "I love you. These are easy words to say, yet my heart fails as I say them, for their meaning is as full and musical as the bell of doom."

We should never tire of expressing love, for certainly we never tire of hearing it expressed. Strange how simple it is for us to use these words with inanimate things. We feel safe in loving our car, a new coat, or spaghetti and meatballs. But we have grave difficulties verbalizing our love for other human beings, even to those closest to us.

In my Love Class I required that each student go home, look their father in the eyes and say, "I love you, Dad." This assignment was the source of immense anxiety. The response from Dad was always surprising, ranging from total shock, a stammered, "I'm glad, but what's with you?" to "I know that. You don't have to tell me."

The message, "I love you," is not something that goes without saying. To the contrary, it needs to be said whenever and wherever love is present.

There is more hunger for love and appreciation
in this world than for bread.
MOTHER TERESA

The art of staying in love

Our library shelves are full of volumes telling us how to win at the game of love. The problem is that most deal with love as a game, but they do not want to be hampered by the rules. Add to that a regrettably large number of people who are unaware that there are rules at all.

Falling in love is easy. In fact, it is so easy that some manage to do so regularly. The passion they call *love* rarely proceeds beyond the glandular stage, or to be more precise, is seldom discerned above the belt. This *love* represents little more than a carnal expression which, once realized, diminishes in force until the next time it is reactivated by a new *love interest.*

Staying in love requires far more of us. To satisfy the senses may be the major challenge for some, but it is actually the easiest part. The mind and spirit require continual attention and stimulation as well. It is not until we assume responsibility for the enhancement of the total self that love can survive.

You can work at something for twenty years and come away with
twenty years worth of valuable experience, or you can come
away with one year's experience twenty times.
GWEN JACKSON

Love and perfection

Human perfection is an illusion. No one is perfect, no thing is perfect. In art, it is usually the flaw that makes the masterpiece more intriguing.

Striving to do our best is what life is all about. The problem lies in the misguided belief that we will not be loved unless we reach the highest levels of achievement. Such beliefs create compulsive behaviors which only sap our energies, getting us nowhere.

This notion is so extreme that some people will threaten suicide because they burned the pot roast. Others will make the joy of gardening a mad obsession because they are determined to have the most manicured lawn in the neighborhood. These people behave as if mistakes or small imperfections are permanent, irreversible stains on their carefully cultivated images.

Few die from imperfection. Most are allowed to try again, improving decisions and behaviors. We don't have to always be right.

When we relinquish the neurotic need to be perfect, we are freed of the pressures of sainthood and can learn from our mistakes instead of being destroyed by them.

If you haven't forgiven yourself something,
how can you forgive others?
DOLORES HUERTA

*L*asting love

There is a great deal of "how to" literature about keeping love alive that can be distilled into two words: persistent effort. When we are held back, pushed aside, ignored, hurt, rejected, we must be like the heart that keeps beating even in the damaged body; we must persist. If we are not prepared to be resilient in love, we need to be prepared for a short relationship!

Nearly everyone is guilty of having thrown up their hands in despair over some seemingly loveless act or unsolvable problem in relating. Every attempt at rectifying the situation seemed to push us into another dizzying failure until we finally lost the motivation, if not the reason, to try once more.

Since we cannot live without love, we must rise up and try again. It helps if we keep in mind that there are few obstacles that can resist perseverance, determination, patience, and most of all, more love.

It's not whether you get knocked down.
It's whether you get up again.
VINCENT LOMBARDI

Live now, dissect later

Everyone is preoccupied with trying to figure out what life is all about. By the time they figure it out, the show is over.

There is an old story about a seeker who has traveled high into the Himalayas to find a great teacher whom he believes has the secret of life. After much hardship, the traveler finally comes face to face with the wise one in a cave high in the mountains. The seer has been a recluse for many years, half naked, dressed in only a few dirty rags. His face and head are a tangled mass of snowy hair. His eyes are red and glassy from lack of sleep.

The traveler sits nervously at the teacher's side. "Tell me," he pleads, "What is the secret of life?"

"The secret of life is simple," responds the teacher. "Life is just a bowl of cherries."

The traveler is startled by the teacher's response. "A bowl of cherries!" he exclaims.

The teacher ponders this for a moment and then questions, "You mean it isn't?"

Life is what is happening while we waste precious time pondering what life is all about.

Minds are like parachutes:
they function only when they are open.
ANONYMOUS

Listening is love
in action.

Separateness is an illusion

Everything is interconnected. It is said that not a leaf falls or a child is left to suffer without each of us somehow being affected. We have finally come to accept the fact that it is a small world which is becoming perceptibly smaller all the time. There is no longer a place to hide from each other.

No wall is high or strong enough to separate us from one another's loneliness or despair. Even if we convince ourselves that we do not need other people, they need us.

Love is the most effective connection to all things. It has the power to enlighten, heal, unite, enrich and restore. All we need do is be open to it.

Just as the wave cannot exist for itself, but must always participate
in the swell of the ocean, so we can never experience life
by ourselves, but must always share the experience
of life that takes place all around us.
ALBERT SCHWEITZER

The prudent know love

The conventional view of love is that it is mainly a thing of the heart, an intangible something that often overpowers us with indescribable emotions. The Lakota Indians, on the other hand, believe that love is the first wisdom given to us and that all things are derived from that knowledge.

When we talk of love at first sight between two people, we can only hope for their sake that it involved foresight as well. Whatever brought them together will keep them together only if they are determined to continually enhance their knowledge of each other. Love must be growing if it is to be enduring. It must be nourished by mutual experience, understanding, patience, judgment and discretion. By its very complex nature, it is continually redefining itself. To accept the changing nature of love is to be true to the mind as well as the heart.

Love is the driving force for the highest values of human life:
to the power of truth, knowledge, beauty, freedom,
goodness and happiness.
PITIRIM SOROKEN

Risking in love

I have heard it said that there is nothing wrong with allowing yourself to get into hot water as long as you emerge cleaner for it. Risk is always worth the effort.

I was told that if I left a good job to travel around the world, I'd be sorry and I'd certainly never be tenured as a professor. I took off anyway. And when I returned, I found an even better job and was tenured in spite of my decision.

I was told that if I taught a Love Class at the university, which I felt was strongly needed, I'd be considered a nut. I taught the Love Class anyway, was indeed considered a nut, and the class changed my entire life for the better.

When I was small, I was informed often enough that dreams don't come true for people who live on the wrong side of the tracks. I was told that I'd never get to college and would do better to lower my sights toward more realistic goals. But I continued to dream and set my goals anyway. I not only went to college, but graduated with a doctorate.

I've never given up a single dream.

Everything worthwhile is a risk. To play it safe is to miss the point of the game. Certainly, risk brings with it the possibility of pain, but there is a more profound pain that comes from the emptiness of never having risked at all. Certainly, no one who has ever succeeded in love has ever played it safe.

It's kind of fun to do the impossible.
WALT DISNEY

Healthy love thrives on differences

People who expect to receive in exact measure the degree of love they give are due for serious disappointments. Love isn't weighed and dispensed in equal measures. Because we all enter into our relationships as persons with different histories, resources and knowledge, we bring varied possibilities, strengths and weaknesses to these relationships. One partner may be more nurturing, another less demonstrative; one is more insecure, the other more stable, and so on. It is not possible, nor even desirable, that two people completely balance each other. Imbalance creates the challenge and motivation for growth. Seen this way, differences have the potential to unite, though they are too often expected to do just the opposite.

It is part of the wonder of love that people can be united hopelessly, madly, totally in love, and still follow their own heart beat.

A life lived in love will never be dull.
L.F.B.

Make love an art

Many of us have an armchair view of love. We create a fixed, comfortable parameter for our feelings and sit back safely within these self-imposed limits. We don't go to love, we expect it to come to us. We look to novels, movies and television to bring us to love vicariously, content to be passive observers. We are fearful of emotions that make demands on us, that can possibly get out of hand.

Love is not known to thrive in such an atmosphere. Real lovers do more than just seek the comfort of love, they strive to make it an art. They are fully aware that this will require a continuous expanding of their senses and sharpening of their perceptions in order to keep up with the challenge of love.

Love is a vast canvas awaiting our artistic expression. The work is never really completed, it's always a work in progress. But as with all creative endeavors, as we labor, we are treated to a broader vision, a keener insight, and the joy that comes mainly from the artistic process itself, less concerned with critical judgment and the finished masterpiece.

Loving, like prayer, is a power as well as a process.
It's curative. It is creative.
ZONA GALE

*A*ssertiveness and loving

Recent self-help literature has abundantly reassured us of our right to be assertive. It tells us that we all should be who we are, say what we feel, and within societal limits, do our own thing. We are encouraged to speak our minds without submission and timidity. But some people have interpreted this to mean that they have a right to be brutally honest and generally obnoxious as long as it furthers their ends. This behavior is based upon the premise that timidity gets you nothing and nowhere.

We don't have to attack to be assertive. In fact, effective assertiveness is most often courteous, kind and gentle. It makes a point without bludgeoning another person into submission.

To be assertive in the positive sense, we strive for a balance between standing up for what we believe to be right and what we know to be the rights of others. We must know what it is we want, how we feel and what we think, and state these things simply, openly, without anger or fear.

When a man points a finger at someone else, he should remember
that three of his fingers are pointing at himself.
LOUIS NIZER

Most of us are pawns
in a game of love
we don't understand.

Love's priorities

A successful way to determine how much we truly care for someone is to discern how high their happiness and welfare are on our priority list. This may sound mechanical and arbitrary, but it is a simple and reliable indicator for measuring our love.

We all have personal priorities, whether conscious or not, when it comes to how we apportion our time and the social choices we make. For example, how often do we place our own needs and desires over those of the people we love? Is our lover's desire to attend a dinner party on a specific evening more important than our missing a baseball game, a concert or a night out with the girls or boys? Do we keep loved ones waiting because we consider our time far more valuable than theirs? Just how willing are we to postpone our desires and reorder our priorities for their happiness?

This does not mean that we should be constantly readjusting our lives for the sake of others. It does suggest that we might be more able to judge how much we value our loving relationships by taking an honest look at our behavioral priorities.

To love is to place our happiness in the happiness of another.
GOTTFRIED WILHELM VAN LUBREITZ

You are enough

You are the perfect you. No one can be a better you, no matter how much they so desire. This does not mean that you don't have the potential to become more. It simply means that you are not in competition with anyone. When you truly accept the fact that you have all you need to become fully you, you free yourself from a self-created, artificial identity. To be someone you are not takes inordinate amounts of energy that could better go toward a more productive activity.

Since you are one of a kind, the message here is clear. You have something to offer that will never again be possible. To devalue this is not only a tragedy for you, but, in fact, for the world.

I am only one, but still I am one.
I cannot do everything, but still I can do something.
I will not refuse to do the something I can do.
HELEN KELLER

Love serves as more than a mirror for us

Remove egotism from love and there would be pitifully few lovers. It is said that, like Narcissus, we seek lovers who mirror us. We insist that they continually flatter us, reinforce our beliefs, take pride in our actions and make our welfare paramount.

We see every aspect of love only as it relates to us. We simply bask in this conceit, and are quick to reject anything that does not fit these attitudes and perceptions. If someone dares to disagree with us, or present a differing view of the world, we are certain that they cannot love us. If someone criticizes us, we are quick to label this as unloving behavior. Our vision is blind beyond the "I." We want others to simply be convenient lenses through which we are affirmed.

When we behave in this way, we don't love lovers, we love lovers to love us.

You can make more friends in two months by becoming interested in other people than you can in two years of trying to get other people interested in you.
DALE CARNEGIE

The way to understand is to be understanding

I was intrigued to learn that the derivative of the verb "to understand" is literally, "to observe standing beneath." There is a great deal of wisdom in this. To understand something, you must truly know it fully, from the bottom up.

We human beings love to rush to judgments. We have opinions about everything, even when we don't know anything about the subjects. We spend an inordinate amount of time predicting, estimating, speculating, deciding and criticizing, usually with little or no foundation. Mostly this is true because we are confined in our understanding of things by what we know about ourselves, which can often be very meager indeed.

It follows then that a better understanding of ourselves will bring us closer to an understanding of others. When we are able to accept the often unpredictable ways in which we behave and think, we can begin to see more clearly why others do what they do and think how they think. An old American Indian adage says that we can't understand anyone else until we have spent ample time in their moccasins. To this I would like to add that we should consider being more comfortable in our own moccasins before we try to fit into anyone else's.

The only justification we have to look down on someone is because
we are about to pick him up.
JESSE JACKSON

Love is not love unless it is used

There is seemingly so little love shared in this world, it is not surprising that we ask, "Where have all the lovers gone?" Since love is the most vital energy for good that is within our power to utilize, it is puzzling why we so seldom do so. Love is just a useless, abstract idea until we put it into action.

One misconception about love is that it is finite, that giving too much or too freely depletes our supply. People who believe this are very frugal with their love and spend lifetimes hoarding it, for what I cannot imagine.

What else do we have to give that costs us so little? What else is so inexhaustible in supply? What else confers such benefits to both the giver and the receiver?

Unless we are always actively living in love, we are not utilizing the greatest gift we have been given and which we, in turn, have to offer.

If I can stop one heart from breaking,
I shall not live in vain.
If I can ease one life the aching,
or cool one pain,
or help one fainting robin into his nest again,
I shall not live in vain.
EMILY DICKINSON

We all have the equal potential to love and be loved

We may not all have equal wealth, power, intelligence, or fame, but we all have the equal ability to grow in love. I hear people say that love is easier for the wealthy or powerful or famous because they have more time to devote to its well being. The average person, on the other hand, is perceived to be more concerned with basic survival than with nonessential romantic concepts such as love.

In reality, everyone knows at heart that money, power, fame, and intelligence have little or no relationship to success in love. Money can buy sex, even fleeting moments of respect, but not love. Power can motivate, intimidate, coerce, but it cannot assure love. Famous people have their well-publicized problems with love, in spite of the fact that their fame can be a very attractive asset. And even those among us with the highest I.Q.s are not always wise when it comes to love.

Of all human behaviors, love is the most steadfastly democratic. How successful we are is determined mostly by how much we are willing to dedicate ourselves to the process of learning to love, how resilient we are to our failures, how daring we are with our lives, how flexible we are with our attitudes, and how amenable we are to change.

Each of us will one day be judged by our standard of life . . .
not by our standard of living; by our measure of giving . . .
not by our measure of wealth; by our simple goodness . . .
not by our seeming greatness.
WILLIAM ARTHUR WARD

Bitterness only ends up souring

No one seeks out bitter fruit. The same is true with bitter people.

Not long ago I received a letter from a woman who was complaining about her loneliness. She explained that she had been abandoned by her husband. Her family, she wrote, visited her only on rare occasions, and always reluctantly when they did. She continued with a catalogue of complaints. She was bitter about her advancing age, her failing health, about the uncaring world, about unloving friends. She was angry even with those who seemed to want to help her. She saw her bitterness as justified in every case and was unaware of the role that her unceasing negativity was playing in furthering her isolation.

When I responded to her letter by hinting that her negative attitudes might be contributing to her problem (after all, who would want to be a part of such bitterness?) she wrote back that I was even worse than the others since I was purporting to be a lover and was, in reality, nothing but a hypocrite.

Experience tells us that we get back from life pretty much what we give. If we turn a bitter face to the world, for whatever reason, we can expect little else in return. If, however, we face adversity with a sense of humor and hold to a base of gratitude for what we have, we're likely to find people responding to us in kind.

He always had a chip on his shoulder that he was ready
to use to kindle an argument.
FRED ALLEN

Love is not for the
easily defeated
or the quickly
disillusioned.

An ounce of discretion is worth more than a pound of knowledge

Italian Proverb

Children require immediate resolution for their frustration. If they don't receive it, they use a whole repertoire of stomping, crying behavior to get their way. As we grow older, we hopefully, if painfully, learn that the world was not created solely for us. Other people need and deserve our consideration. We learn about tact and discretion and to listen to that little voice inside that says, "Shut up! This is not the time, the place or the reason to go with my impulses." We learn to wait for passions to subside and cooler heads to prevail.

When we truly value another's feelings, we are willing to postpone our desires, repress our demands (at least temporarily), knowing that there is no winning if we've had our say and lost our love.

I have a friend who feels compelled to sound off at the slightest provocation. In defense of this behavior, he cites current theories on the importance of psychological ventilation which say that if anger and frustration are not expressed immediately, irreparable physical and psychological damage will surely result. So you will find him engaged in tirades with family, friends and anyone who may cross his path at the wrong time. He is convinced that this is conducive to his health, never mind what this is doing to the health (particularly the mental health) of those around him. Yet he can't understand why he feels so unwanted, lonely and unloved.

A little selective suppression, even when we're certain we're right, does more than win friends and influence people. It enhances feelings of respect and love and is the stuff of which lasting relationships are made.

With a sweet tongue and kindness,
you can drag an elephant by a hair.
PERSIAN PROVERB

Using love for convenience

The so-called "Me Decade" of the Eighties saw love approached more as a business transaction, with people reduced to commodities. These individuals were more concerned with ego gratification than with mutual satisfaction.

Of course, not everyone identified with this attitude but most of us know of relationships based upon these "me" values, i.e. two people independently, without regard to each other, pursuing their own personal agendas.

Several years back I came to know a woman who seemed to have ordered her husband from a catalogue, so perfect was he for her. He was handsome, intelligent, hardworking, dedicated and loyal—all the better, at the time, to impress her friends and provide her ego gratification. After a few years, she told me that "Mr. Perfect" had lost his luster, much as a dazzling new outfit does when it is repeatedly displayed. She felt little compunction about discarding him and going off in search of a new love. She saw this as a duty to herself. She was soon remarried. He, on the other hand, has yet to recover.

When we use other people as a means to our own ends, we reduce them to the status of objects. It is no surprise when those so used remain damaged and broken for years, if not forever.

Such behavior is a distortion of basic decency. It has nothing to do with love.

What generally saps us and poisons our happiness is that
we feel that we shall soon exhaust and reach
the end of whatever attracts us.
PIERRE TEILHARD DE CHARDIN

Surviving the wounds of love

If we are going to be lovers, we must be as open to the wretchedness as we are to the bliss it can bring, for both are a part of the reality of loving. Since earthly love is imperfect, we will never be able to avoid pain, but the lover finds ways of surviving the wounds. I have often noted that there is no lover worth the name who is not covered with minor scars.

Most individuals outlive their injuries, but there are some who continue to flaunt them like proud battle wounds as they continue their war on love. They keep a sacred list of wrongs that burn in memory as a warning to never let it happen again.

Love may bring disappointments and devastation, but it is the wise among us who learn from them. Having done so makes love's triumphs even sweeter. Our emotional strength and growth toward wisdom develop over a lifetime, and quite often, arise out of adversity. This is a small price to pay for such powerful knowledge.

Adversity not only draws people together, but brings forth that beautiful inward friendship, just as the cold winter forms ice figures on window panes, which the warmth of the sun effaces.
SÖREN KIERKEGAARD

Publicizing love

So much of our lives are overrun by hate, greed, violence and selfishness that we are tempted to overlook the fact that there is at least an equal amount of goodness in the world. The problem is that those who promote their negativity and hate seem to be far more vocal than the lovers and are certainly given more media time.

For years I have been promoting a television series celebrating good people doing good things. I have been told by the experts to forget it, that goodness doesn't sell! Positive stories, like good people, it would seem, lack appeal. As a result, we are developing a whole generation which devalues loving one another and is drawn more to a negative view of life, to which it refers as the "real world."

It's not surprising that so many people are enticed by hate and violence and selfishness the way our society glorifies it. It seems to me that there has never been a more important time for us to fearlessly publicize goodness and display love, at any cost.

We suffer from seeing too much death and not enough life, too much sorrow and not enough joy, too much greed and not enough giving, too much loneliness and not enough love.
ANONYMOUS

Dying comes naturally to us all, having the courage to live does not

Life is ours to do with as we will. We can accept what comes with a sad sort of resignation, or we can rage against it with human passion. We can find life as exaltation or subjugation, as cause for bliss or despondency, ecstasy or emptiness. The point is that the choice is ours!

My mother had the most positive view of life I have ever known. When things went badly, she immediately set out to put it into perspective. Instead of brooding or cursing her fate, she would invite friends over for a good pasta. (Pasta cured every ill!) At other times, she would plan an outing, usually to the sea, which she saw as very healing. In this way, she reminded herself (and us) of the pleasures that life could bring instead of concentrating on its grim offerings. She lived to be 82 years old and never lost this quality. She convinced us all that it was always better to choose life, especially, as Woody Allen says, when you consider the alternative.

Be glad of life because it gives you the chance to love and to work and to play and to look up at the stars.
HENRY VAN DYKE

Affection and love

Ours is one of the few societies where physical contact, even in family and with friends, is not encouraged or celebrated. In our large Italian family, not to hug and kiss was considered punishable behavior.

Science has proven that a simple hug is one of the most convenient and inexpensive therapies available. Yet we remain touch starved. In a study I did for my book, LOVING EACH OTHER, respondents mentioned three qualities which they considered essential for happy, long-lasting relationships. It was rather surprising to find that affection (touching, holding, stroking) was named most important by the majority of the respondents, second only to communication. Sex, on the other hand, which they separated from affection, was relegated to eighth position.

Affection, nonsexual touching, is a tremendous resource of both physical and emotional well being and essential to growth in love. It is free, you need no special equipment and it is always available. To love we must let people know we care. The best way is to literally reach out and show them as often as possible.

Loving touch makes the difference.
Without Mom's chicken soup, without Mother Teresa,
without the loving touch of our neighbor in church or a caress in
the hospital, we might as well live like animals.
EVERETT TETLEY

Rigidity and love

Learning is a wonderful thing. We are, for the most part, freer and happier because of it. But while learning can liberate, it can also entrap. We acquire our basic system of beliefs and values early in life. These old mindsets can invalidate new perceptions and perpetuate useless stereotypes. One of the stunning rewards of loving someone is that he or she can help us to see things in new ways by challenging our beliefs and behaviors. Love invites us to broaden our perspectives by allowing us to see the world through the eyes of another. We miss the point when we see this challenge as a threat to our integrity rather than an exciting source for our growth.

Love alone is capable of uniting living beings in such a way as to complete and fulfill them, for it alone takes them and joins them by what is deepest in themselves.
PIERRE TEILHARD DE CHARDIN

Love is earned

The more we attempt to demand love, the more it eludes us. No pleading, promising, bartering, cajoling or threatening can secure love. True love will only be given when earned.

Love withers under constraint; its very essence is liberty; it is
compatible neither with obedience, jealousy, nor fear: it
is there most pure, perfect and unlimited, where its
votaries live in confidence, equality and reserve.
PERCY BYSSHE SHELLEY

Ego as a barrier to love

Most of us think we are lovers, but few of us ever get outside of ourselves long enough to know what that truly means. "To love" means to move the focus from us to others and set as our major goal helping them to realize their God-given potential. In their success we find pride; in their growth we find satisfaction; in their increased knowledge we are wiser by being able to share it. Through relinquishing our egos from time to time we move closer to others and to an understanding of love.

One nice thing about egoists:
they don't talk about other people.
LUCILLE S. HARPER

Looking at love

We may have 20/20 vision, but few of us ever bother to use it.

I received a letter from a woman who wrote, "I don't think my husband has really looked at me for the last fifteen years. We're seldom apart, yet I think I could come into a room stark naked on a white horse, with my hair on fire and he'd go right on watching TV or reading the paper. It's not that he doesn't love me, it's just that I've become the invisible woman."

When I was teaching Love Class, I would say to my students, "You've lived with your mother for over twenty years. What color are her eyes?" Amazingly, few could answer the question with any degree of certainty.

We miss seeing our children as they grow up. People we love, die; and a few weeks later we have great difficulties picturing them.

I recall speaking to a large conference of blind and partially sighted people. After my talk, one of the participants came up to me and asked if she could "Braille" me. With soft, caring fingers, she surveyed my face as her eyes could not do. When she finished, she smiled in a most delightful manner and said, "How nice."

A very large part of communication is nonverbal. When words deceive and eyesight fails, it's good to remember that we perceive love fully through *all* of our senses.

There are none so blind as they who will not see.
ANONYMOUS

The only lasting trauma is the one we suffer without positive change.

A time for joy

It's strange how we seem determined to keep a record of the bad things in life while so readily forgetting the good.

In Love Class, I made it an assignment that each student share a peak experience of despair and a peak experience of joy. It was bewildering to me how easily people related their despair (often in detail) and how difficult it was for them to recall joyous times. Perhaps it is not so astonishing when we think of how our lives are bombarded with news of devastation and hopelessness. The history that we all studied in school is almost exclusively a chronicle of wars, oppression, famines, and catastrophes. There is little record of happiness and peace.

Mama used to encourage us to collect as many memories of happiness as we could. She assured us that they would come in handy during the times when things were not going so well. And she practiced what she preached. When hard times struck, she would remind us that there were happier days ahead. She also had a wonderful talent of turning painful experiences into positive ones. One occasion comes instantly to mind. Papa informed us one evening that his business partner had absconded with their funds leaving him bankrupt and deeply in debt. Of course, our whole family was distressed by this news. How would we pay our bills? Where would we get our next meal? The following evening Mama answered that last question. She prepared the most elaborate feast we had seen in months. Papa was furious. "Have you gone crazy?" he angrily demanded. "No," Mama replied, "I just thought it was a perfect time for celebration. This is when we need to be happy the most! We'll survive." And survive we did. In addition to a practical lesson, Mama also gave us all a beautiful memory which has served us well over these many years. No one in our family will ever forget that dinner.

Keep a record of the times you've triumphed over misfortune. It will assure you that you can do so again. Remember your moments of joy and happiness. They will serve as a reservoir of strength when you most need it.

Know that there are always causes for celebration in the best of times; but perhaps more importantly, also remember in the worst of times.

Learn to laugh at your troubles and you'll
never run out of things to laugh at.
LYN KAROL

It is impossible to solve our problems while remaining the same person who brought them on

No person or relationship is free of problems. When they do occur, it is well to remember that we, ourselves, are responsible for them, at least in part. We may even have been their source. When we continue to approach our conflicts in the same old way, we drift further from the possibilities of a permanent solution. We simply continue to trudge on our personal treadmills, going nowhere, solving nothing.

Ideally, overcoming conflicts is all about adding new insights and acquiring new skills. When we approach obstacles as opportunities for making ourselves over, we not only find solutions, but we immeasurably enhance our general problem-solving abilities as well.

The next best thing to solving a problem is
finding some humor in it.
FRANK A. CLARK

*R*apt attention as the message of love

A student of my Love Class once told me that there were times when she felt that the entire world was deaf to the sound of her voice. "I get no response. I speak and end up feeling that I am talking to myself. Am I going mad?"

I assured her that she was not, and that she was also not the only one who felt this. Most of us have experienced the emptiness that comes from feeling tuned out. Listening is an act of love, or at a more basic level, an act of simple consideration.

All communication requires two basic things, a speaking voice and a listening ear. This sounds pretty simple, but it's not. Most of us are very selective listeners, tuning in and tuning out as our interest dictates. With all the extraneous noise and worthless static that bombards us daily, this skill can be a blessing. It is something else, however, when we find ourselves tuning out those we say we love.

Over the years, as attention fades, as more distractions intrude and voices grow dimmer, a deaf ear is too often turned to the ones who most need to be heard. And then, as so often happens, when we realize what we've done and try to tune back in, it's too late.

We have two ears and only one tongue in order
that we may hear more and speak less.
DIOGENES

The compulsion to change those we love

How often we find fault with those we love. We think that if only they could be more of this or less of that, or more like this one and less like that one, then our love would be fulfilled. This is true even when part of the problem stems from our own whims, our own peculiar moods, or plainly, our own stupidity.

One of my favorite letters was from a woman who was determined to change her husband (even before he was her husband). After years of nagging, threatening, molding and shaping, she finally succeeded. At long last he was all that she wished him to be. Now she had a new problem. She complained that he was no longer the man she married.

People have one thing in common: they are all different.
ROBERT ZEND

When love needs help

We have all been nurtured on the myth of romantic love where, in the closing pages, it is suggested that all troubles, conflicts and anxieties cease once lovers fall into a warm embrace where they remain entwined in a blissful forever. Two now have become one, inseparable and perfect for eternity.

This is the basis of the "happy ever aftering" syndrome which has us applauding the ecstatic side of passion and romance and all but neglecting the practical, patient, more peaceful side. And so the years go by and we find ourselves looking back upon the wonder of how we were and inflicting impossible expectations of some nebulous perfection upon each other.

Just as life passes through many changes, so does love. The more we are expecting, accepting and welcoming of these changes, the more secure our love.

People who matter are most aware that everyone else does, too.
MALCOLM S. FORBES

*T*rust

Trust is one of the most basic qualities of love. We need to know that we are safe, that others want our well being, and that they desire us to grow. We crave the knowledge that people are for us. Until we receive this message from others, we are less open to their influence and we become, in turn, less concerned about their welfare.

We are forever putting people to the test to see whether they truly love us or not. We watch to see if they are thoughtful, if they give themselves freely or if they hold back, if they are listening to us with their hearts as well as their minds, if they are sharing our happiness or being threatened by it, if they are willing to stand by us when we need them or abandon us at the least sign of conflict. Once we are certain of their love, anything becomes possible. We are encouraged to grow and risk beyond our imagined limitations. We find the strength to overcome our fears or break self-destructive habits. We see our way to giving up grudges or expressing repressed feelings or even offering a painful apology. These minor miracles all become possible when we are secure and trust in love.

When you have nothing left but love,
then for the first time you become aware that love is enough.
ANONYMOUS

Many of us get our emotional exercise by jumping to negative conclusions.

Love is not a private affair

Though each of us may be but one person among millions, we are all powerful forces for good or evil. Everything on this earth has its purpose, its reason and its effect. Like the pebble thrown into the pond, every act we perform spreads out in ever widening circles, embracing everything in its growing path.

It may be difficult to understand the concept that all things are interconnected and that, as such, whatever happens affects us all in some real way. It follows, therefore, that whatever good or evil we do is not a private affair. It is important to us all.

As long as there is pain, suffering, loneliness, and hunger in this world, it is our responsibility. There is no place for an exclusive, provincial love when the effects of our caring, giving and loving have the power to change the lives of the people we love. By these acts we change the world as well.

If you think you have given enough, think again.
There is always more to give and someone to give it to.
NORMAN VINCENT PEALE

Keeping fear in balance

No one is immune to fear. But as with all emotions, it needs to be kept in balance with opposing voices that urge us to take chances, to be more adventurous, to risk.

The first time we wobbled on a bicycle we became acutely aware of the prospects of suffering physical pain. It served to make us more tentative because we appreciated the risk involved. But the joy of learning to ride was stronger than the fear of danger, so we practiced the skills necessary until the fear was overcome by the joy. Uncomplicated loving behaviors such as smiling at someone, initiating a conversation, offering a compliment, expressing an honest emotion, are all things we fear only because we don't practice them enough. If by putting them into action we bruise our egos a little in the process, it's really not much different from the skinned knee we acquired from learning to ride the bicycle and which soon healed and was forgotten. Love requires that we overcome the irrational and self-defeating fears that inevitably place distance between us and others.

On this earth, though far and near,
without love, there's only fear.
PEARL S. BUCK

Striving to be loved,
rather than striving to love

We expect to be loved and are quick to condemn those who do not comply. We believe that life comes with a guarantee that we will be loved. It rarely occurs to us that the degree to which we are loved is directly related to our lovability.

We are all acquainted with individuals who are constantly moody, who look for the dark side of everything, who are fearful of commitment, who shirk from responsibility, who flare up at the least provocation and then wonder why they are not sought after, why they are not loved. Who would love such a person except someone who is asking for unhappiness?

It is when we ask for love *less* and begin giving it *more* that the basis of human love is revealed to us.

What can pay love, but love?
MARY DE LA RIVIÈRE MANLEY

74

Looking for a love that doesn't exist

We all go about with visions of the perfect love. Some of us feel that, at the very least, it is what we merit. We fantasize relationships without conflict, brimming with warmth and understanding, acceptance and tenderness. We spend a great deal of time measuring what we have against our dreams of what we feel we deserve, bemoaning what is lacking.

I have a friend who was so obsessed with finding the perfect lover that he left his wife and child to set upon his quest to do so. He saw this as his right to happiness. Since making this decision, he brags that he has courted at least seventeen women, but has yet to find the ideal he is seeking. When asked what he is so desperately searching for in a relationship, he replies that he is looking for true love. Of course, he has no real idea of what that means. It seems to me that he won't be content until he marries himself.

Perhaps we would feel less frustrated if we could accept the fact that on this earth there is no perfect love, only human love. Then we could expend our energies appreciating and enhancing the love we have.

We can only learn to love by loving.
IRIS MURDOCH

When we relinquish our dignity we also relinquish our right to complain about it

It's always easier to blame others for any pain or frustration we feel. We are seldom willing to accept the responsibility for our own unhappiness. In examining our behavior carefully and honestly, we might find that through our own indifference, weakness or ignorance, we have performed the unforgivable: we have relinquished control of ourselves to someone else. We've given up the most vital component of love. Is it any wonder, then, that we feel empty and dead? Overwhelmed and cowered, we have become a no-thing. And, worst of all, we have permitted it to happen.

Our happiness is based in a large part on our sense of dignity. Without self-respect, without some sense of self-worth (which is our birthright), we are diminished in our ability to give or receive anything, let alone such a valued gift as love.

Man is what he believes.
ANTON CHEKHOV

Possessiveness always ends by destroying what it tries to protect

Absolute control over another human being is neither possible nor desirable. It is always destructive. One of the great myths about true love is that it means two people's lives are forever intertwined, set upon the same path, having the same goals and interests and that every moment away from one another should seem like an eternity. Even if this were possible, it sounds terribly dull to me.

It is only natural to want to share ourselves intimately, to want to feel protected and close. It only becomes a problem when we need it to be an exclusive, full-time arrangement. Those who focus their love on only one person have a problem with caring in general.

It should be a relief rather than a threat to find that those we love have a capacity for loving others as well as being loved. We can be thankful that they have interests apart from us, that they are self-sufficient and self-reliant.

We really are capable of loving many people at the same time without diluting what we have to give. In fact, the more loving experiences we have, the more we have to bring with us when we focus on a deep, intimate relationship. The quality of love is not strained when it is shared; rather it is intensified and most assuredly improves with the experience.

And stand together, yet not too near together.
For the pillars of the temple stand apart, and the oak tree and
cypress grow not in each others' shadow.
KAHLIL GIBRAN

Viable alternatives in loving

Too often when we are confronted with a problem, we seek the perfect solution. This is only a blueprint for frustration, which more likely drives us to distraction than action.

Every problem has as many solutions as there are creative individuals dealing with it. Let us say, for example, that John has assured Mary that he would call her at precisely three o'clock. By two, Mary's heart is all ready to receive it. By three, she is feeling anxiety. By three thirty, she is feeling frustration. By four, she is angry. By five, she is furious and in tears. By six, she is prepared to commit murder or suicide. Her distress is consuming her every thought and her imagination is running wild.

Gone from her mind, though, are the many alternatives with which to handle the situation. She could call John. Better yet, she could call Pete. She could call a girlfriend and suggest a movie. She could make a pizza and invite friends in to share it. She could write a poem or a letter expressing her frustration. She could hand out daisies to the neighbors. She could visit a friend in a hospital. My point is simple. Our problems always have more than one solution.

Too many times I've seen people staggered and defeated by a problem they were unwilling to approach from a different viewpoint. What is at stake is nothing less than having the personal dignity and freedom it takes to direct our own lives. Happily, the choice is ours. The healthy individual is one who has the most viable alternatives available for whatever conflicts present themselves.

It isn't that they can't see the solution.
It is that they can't see the problem.
G.K. CHESTERTON

Life lived for
tomorrow will always
be just a day away
from being realized.

*G*etting along

If a valued truism is overused, it can easily be dismissed as a trite platitude. So it is with the sound counsel, "Do unto others as you would have them do unto you." If we have become jaded by such advice, we might call it simple consideration, selflessness, empathy or love. No matter how the idea is stated, it is still the basis of all positive interactive behavior. When we treat others as we would like to be treated, we are at least creating a basis for living together in peace. From that very solid beginning, we can agree to cooperate, adapt, compromise and share. We become willing to relinquish our petty needs to a greater good and put aside immediate gratification for long term goals.

We question why there is so much dissension, deceit and fear in the world, yet we fail to examine our own behavior for part of the answer. If the dominant theme of our lives has been "What's in it for me?" we might begin to ask a more essential question, "What am I able to do for others?"

If we can only keep in mind that every person we meet is fighting his or her own battle for love and survival and deserves whatever kindness we have to give, we will be doing our part, regardless of how small, toward alleviating some of this world's distress.

Two things fill my mind with ever new and increasing
wonder and awe: the starry heavens above me
and the moral law within me.
IMMANUEL KANT

We get what we give and find what we expect

It is unfortunate, but nonetheless true, that we live in a world of too many cynics and skeptics. They are a vigilant group, only too eager to expose the insincerity and dishonesty they are certain is common to all. They are convinced that acts of kindness and love are mostly a result of ulterior motives.

Many of us, unfortunately, have fallen prey to developing a hard outer shell. If someone offers us a rose and immediately follows up with a plea for a donation, we naturally form a mind set against such future occurrences. From that time on, every flower offered is cause for suspicion.

Lovers who have trusted and made themselves vulnerable in a relationship may suddenly find that they have been deceived. When they pick up the pieces, and are again offered love, they are understandably skeptical. They have become "healthy cynics"—less open, less trusting, less vulnerable; in short, less able to maintain healthy relationships in the future.

It is far easier, it seems to me, to become a cynic than it is to work beyond disappointments and rise above wounds. We must be willing to trust again and expect better than we've received. True cynics who believe they have become experts at seeing through people have actually succumbed to a different kind of blindness. If we want love, it is better to look for the good in people, even if it means being somewhat of a cock-eyed optimist.

There isn't any formula or method.
You learn to love by loving.
ALDOUS HUXLEY

The loving compliment

Mark Twain once said he could go for two months on a good compliment. The most loving compliment I've ever heard of was given by Joseph Choate, former ambassador to Great Britain. When asked who he would like to be if he could come back to earth again after he died, he replied without an instant's hesitation, "Mrs. Choate's second husband."

Nearly every one of us is starving to be appreciated, to be the recipient of that most supreme compliment—that we are loved. We need others to recognize our strengths or sometimes just to prop us up in the places where we tend to lean a little. Honest compliments are simple and cost nothing to give, but we must not underestimate their worth.

The applause of a single human being is of great consequence.
SAMUEL JOHNSON

One is never too old for love

Growing old is seldom anticipated with pleasure once we leave our teens. Perhaps our own attitudes about aging make us apprehensive. My feeling is that it is not age or death we fear as much as the potential for loneliness and lack of affection we see as a possibility. What we fear is a day when our loved ones stop planning with us and start planning for us. A receding hairline, wrinkled skin and a slower pace are not the real reasons many of us dread old age. More accurately, it is the possibility of losing love.

Old age doesn't have to be a cushion of stored memories of love to be rested upon in the afterglow of a full life. We remain loving persons with the same needs as always despite an outer shell that might suggest otherwise. We will need to love and be loved until the day we die.

As long as one can admire and love, then one is young forever.
PABLO CASALS

The paradox of hurting those we love

It is a paradox of love that we often hurt the most the ones we love the most. We are continually correcting their faults, questioning their decisions, challenging their assumptions. We sometimes even place higher standards upon them than we do upon ourselves. There is nothing wrong with wanting those we love to be their best, but we'll never accomplish this with a steady stream of negative criticism.

A few years ago, we did a video analysis of a teacher as she interacted in her classroom. Upon studying the results, we found much to her surprise, that though she cared deeply about her students, her demeanor toward them was almost entirely negative—lists of "thou shalt nots" were everywhere, red penciled papers were returned highlighting wrong responses, and her verbal comments most often were used to point out the children's shortcomings.

Criticism is a complex, subtle art not to be taken or given lightly. It can be constructive, but it can also tear down. The next time we are tempted to say, "The trouble with you is . . . ," we may want to reconsider and ask ourselves why we're doing it! Is there truly a positive reason for making this comment or might it be better to remain silent? What will we have profited if we make our point, but diminish a human being or lose a lover?

Love lights more fire than hate extinguishes.
ELLA WHEELER WILCOX

*L*ove and enthusiasm

Adults envy children. They seem so naturally curious and enthusiastic about everything. Most of us can recall our feelings from childhood. Who can forget a time when we could be sprawled out on the grass for an hour, completely absorbed in the movements of a bug burrowing through the earth or a cloud formation passing overhead. We didn't have to worry about being entertained when there were so many things to invite our curiosity and enthusiasm.

We often become less impressed with life as we grow older. We seem to encounter more bored grownups yawning their way through life with seemingly nothing left to be excited about.

I am pleased to report that it is not necessary to revert to childhood to reignite our enthusiasm for life. All that is needed is to reclaim that small part of ourselves that finds joy in the commonplace and adventure in each moment. It may be buried under a thick crust of gloom, but it is still very much alive within us all.

I'm passionately involved in life. I love its change, its color,
its movements. To be able to speak, to see, to hear, to walk,
to have music and paintings ... it is all a miracle.
ARTHUR RUBINSTEIN

Knowledge comes
by way of ignorance,
so we ought to be
encouraged by what
we don't know.

Need breeds success

There is an old adage which states that if we desire something strongly enough, it's ours for the taking—where there's a will, there's a way. If you are lonely, you can do certain things to alleviate it. If you are experiencing conflicts in loving, you can take steps to solve them. We have the power to improve, but we must also have the will. Solutions can come on the heels of need, but they do not materialize on their own. They arise from a deep desire to really *do* something.

I receive anguished letters from lovers who cry out in despair about their inability to form and maintain lasting relationships. They desperately seek solutions from me, from Dear Abby, from therapists and ministers, but they do nothing. Their excuse is that they are unable to make decisions. They claim to be at their wit's end, clutching at straws, without a clue, at a dead end, helpless, hopeless—so many convenient words and phrases to confirm their powerlessness. In reality, they simply lack the essential determination to get out of their quandry. Though they assert their need to do something, they are unwilling to make the required adjustments, compromises and perhaps even sacrifices necessary to attain their goal.

Love is always there for the taking. The question is, do we really want it badly enough to do the soul searching and hard work necessary to acquire it, or are we just kidding ourselves?

You can have anything you want . . . if you want it badly enough.
You can be anything you want to be, have anything you desire,
accomplish anything you set out to accomplish . . . if you
will hold to that desire with singleness of purpose.
ROBERT COLLIER

The put down

There is little that is more destructive and demeaning than the casual put down. We have become so accustomed to dealing with them that we often fail to realize how devastating they can be in the long-run.

Love enhances, it does not degrade. Love builds self-esteem, it does not diminish it. It is surprising that there are so many who purport to love, yet continue to belittle others. I have never forgotten a woman who said to her husband, who at every opportunity used her as the object of his degrading humor, "If I'm so bad and worthless, why did you marry me?" Good question.

Put downs that attempt to change someone's behavior usually manage to aggravate it. There are so many ways to positively influence behavior. Why do we resort to one that wounds and even has the power to destroy?

The thoughtless are rarely wordless.
HOWARD W. NEWTON

Love discards labels

Emerson, speaking of a simple weed, called it "a plant whose virtues have not yet been discovered." I wonder how many people we have written off as weeds because, for some lame reason or another, they appeared unworthy of our love and attention? The people with whom we become involved, whom we choose to be close to, are obviously personal choices, which is as it should be. It seems to me, though, that our world would be far more interesting and less limiting if we looked more analytically into the labels and excuses we use to distance ourselves from others. If we did, we would likely find that these convenient classifications are based upon outdated tapes that play over and over again in our heads.

In our efforts to fit people into convenient categories, we end up minimizing their worth or excluding them without thoughtful reason. We use age, sex, social standing, monetary status, color, religion, nationality . . . any number of things to distance ourselves from those who are different. This, of course, saves us the trouble of thinking independently and evaluating each individual as a separate, distinct and deserving person. It's very likely that most of the people we meet are worthy of more consideration than we give them. Who knows? Perhaps we may be surprised to find that they are not weeds after all, but rather flowers we've failed to stop long enough to appreciate.

The mind of the bigot is like the pupil of the eye;
the more light you pour upon it, the more it will contract.
OLIVER WENDELL HOLMES, JR.

Love is ageless

Love has nothing to do with age. People don't grow old merely by living a certain number of years. Aging is an activity of the mind, an attitude. We grow old when we give up our sense of fun. We age when we relinquish our ideals, our dignity, our hope, our belief in miracles. Age comes when we cease reveling in the game of life, when we are no longer excited by the new and challenged by the dream. As long as we celebrate the richness of the world, hear the laughter in the voice of love and continue to believe in ourselves, age is incidental.

Love is the long-sought Fountain of Youth. As long as we love, we remain young. Death becomes simply the final stage of development in life. It is well to remember that we are transient guests on earth. Less than a century is not long to live, but it is long enough to learn that love is what it's all about.

May you live all the days of your life.
JONATHAN SWIFT

Necessary anxiety

We have come to believe that anxiety is a state to be avoided at any cost, that it is a deterrent to a constructive and productive lifestyle.

In reality, anxiety has a positive value, within limits. In our own complex world it cannot be avoided, but by manifesting itself as a state of uneasiness, apprehension or concern, it can serve to prepare and alert us to possible problems prior to their occurrence. It is impossible to think of any but the simplest of actions not preceded by some degree of healthy anxiety. Like physical pain, it acts as a warning system which precedes positive action. It is only when we allow anxiety to overpower our reason that problems arise. But when we see it as a normal, human state, it can represent the first step from which all acts of psychic growth and survival build.

Problems are only opportunities in work clothes.
HENRY J. KAISER

A lesson in love from Aunt C. and Uncle L.

As a child I was told repeatedly the story of the courtship of Uncle L. and Aunt C. During the year before they were married, they knew each other only from the letters they exchanged across an ocean. He had been in America for several years; she had lived all her life in a small northern Italian village. My uncle came to know my aunt through her brother, who was a recent immigrant to America, and began to regularly correspond with her. From their letters and a single photograph each sent to the other, came a proposal of marriage and the dream of a better life together.

This resulted in a great love story that lasted for the next fifty-five years. Mama would describe the first time they met and how excited, nervous and uncertain everyone was. I pictured two strangers walking from that train station into a lifelong commitment. Two people who never had the opportunity to fall in love as we usually like to think of it. No ethereal feelings of first love, no infatuation or weak knees or lost appetite, no being swept off one's feet.

Instead there was a simple determination to bring into a marriage what each had to give and share, and make it work. In place of impossible expectations, there was an unspoken understanding that there would be adjustments, and the hope that in time they would grow to love each other—as indeed they did.

Love doesn't just sit there, like a stone.
It has to be made like bread; remade all the time, made new.
URSULA K. LEGUIN

The value of difference

Find the person who will love you because of your differences and not in spite of them and you have found a lover for life.

Happily, we are all individuals similar to others in many ways and yet very different in others. It is these differences that make us who we are and determine the directions in which we will grow and change. Being normal doesn't mean giving up our uniqueness so that we can be like everyone else. It means being proud of the ways in which we are uniquely us. In fact, it is this aspect of ourselves that attracts others and is our most loving gift to them.

If we treat people as they are, they will stay as they are.
But if we treat them for what they might be, and might
become, they will become their better selves.
G.T. SMITH

Life is our greatest
possession and love
its greatest
affirmation.

Love and cultural enrichment

The role of the arts is mainly to enrich our lives, to help us look beyond the usual, to reveal new ways of seeing things, to help us understand the many doorways to the soul.

Life can be pretty grim at times. There are days when we cannot seem to rise above our mundane existence, when we forget that there is more to life than what can be experienced in the limited scope of our minds. So we all need to be reminded that if we stretch our vistas and share new worlds with those we love, we simultaneously enhance our special bonding.

Watching a sunset together, seeing the widening shadows as they bring on the dark of evening, refreshes and renews no matter how often it is experienced. Marveling at geese patterned in flight or noticing the plodding path of a snail enriches us in mysterious ways. Music can also break through the verbal traps we create for ourselves while reaching deep, nonlinguistic levels of consciousness.

Mozart musically colors us delicate. Wagner engulfs us with power. Vivaldi cleanses us. Immersing ourselves in the vast colored canvases of Rothko or the bold vistas of Van Gogh or the golden world of Tintoretto, are universal bridges to our lovers.

It seems a great pity that the genius of so many centuries of creative personkind is all but ignored as a vehicle to unite us more deeply in love when it is so readily ours for the sharing.

Anyone who keeps the ability to see beauty is never old.
FRANZ KAFKA

You are enough

We must be careful not to fall victim to the idea that we are unlovable because we are too much of this and not enough of that. We're fine just the way we are. Diversity is life. There are armies of individuals, for example, who love tall people, or short people, or brunettes, or blonds, or thin people, or heavy people, or silent types, or verbal types, and on and on. The more we are unapologetic about who we are, the more we are assured of lasting love. With patience we discover those who will cherish us. Then we will have a lifetime free of artifice and deception and the freedom to be who we are.

No change brings happiness unless the way it is
effected involves ascent. The happy man is therefore the man who,
without any direct search for happiness, inevitably finds joy
as an added bonus in the act of forging ahead and
attaining the fullness and finality of his own self.
PIERRE TEILHARD DE CHARDIN

Being true to you

For too many of us, being true to ourselves presents difficulties. We fear that, in so doing, we might expose ourselves to ridicule, or worse, rejection. So we play it safe. We create disguises and orchestrate little routines of nonchalance to hide behind. We play the sophisticate or remain aloof, trusting that these facades will shield us from piercing eyes. We do this in spite of our hope that there will be someone who will not accept our artifices. Ironically, the person we are attempting to cover up is precisely the one that others are seeking. The real us is far better than anything we can concoct. The true measure of being loved is that we are not fearful of showing others who we are. In so doing, what we feel we have lost in image, we have gained tenfold in trust and respect.

I recall a novelist describing one of his characters as "not so much a human being as a civil war." Those of us who have fought the battle between who we are and what we feel we must be to be loved, will surely identify with that character.

If we are ever to know love in our lives, we must be willing to reveal ourselves to the people we hold at arm's length, or from whom we have vigorously tried to protect ourselves. Actually, there is nothing to hide.

Oh, the miraculous energy that flows between two people who care enough to get beyond surfaces and games, who are willing to take the risks of being totally open, of listening, of responding with the whole heart. How much we can do for each other.
ALEX NOBLE

*P*atience

Nature offers us an infinite variety of plants that fascinate and delight us. We know that it would be ludicrous for us to pass judgment on them. We don't nag at them to reveal a new bud or leaf when we think they should. Neither do we compare them with other plants in the same garden that we feel are doing so much better. We allow them to do what is natural for them, to grow and flower at their own pace.

It seems logical that the people we love should be offered the same consideration, especially since we cannot be fully aware of the struggles with which they are dealing. Even with the best of intentions, our impatience for them to "grow up" and "be sensible," implies that it's a simple matter. The assumption is that they can and should change at our behest.

I have saved some of my healthiest plants because I learned a long time ago that if I want them to thrive I simply have to allow them to live according to their own nature. Countless times I've given up on some, after having waited patiently for them to respond to my careful nurturing, only to find that one day when they, not I, were quite ready, they unfolded before my eyes. They were simply awaiting their time.

Sometimes our best service to those we love is to simply stand by, be silent, be patient, be hopeful, be understanding, and wait.

The key to everything is patience. You get the
chicken by hatching the egg . . . not by smashing it.
ARNOLD GLASOW

Love frees

Many view commitment in a loving relationship as a giving up or lessening of personal freedom. This may or may not be true, depending upon how one views personal freedom.

Love does assure certain freedoms: the freedom to become angry now and then, even occasionally to completely blow up without fear that it will leave a permanent scar; the freedom to be imperfect, even to the point of making a fool of ourselves without fear that we will lose respect; the freedom to change and thrive, but also to falter or fail, without the fear that we will be abandoned in time of need. Like most of the freedoms we have, these things may be taken for granted. But unlike our other freedoms, they deserve more than a semiannual observance. They should be guarded each and every day.

A love that inhibits is not love. Love is only love when it liberates.

Freedom is nothing else but the chance to be better.
ALBERT CAMUS

Lovers learn not to just hope for the better, they strive to make it happen.

Thankfulness

When I was in elementary school, I had a teacher who we all thought was off her rocker. Each Friday, just prior to the dismissal bell, she would go around the class and ask each of us to name something for which we were thankful. We had to work hard to keep from exploding with laughter as each of my classmates rose to proclaim, "I'm thankful for my bicycle," "I'm thankful for my Shirley Temple doll." And so on.

When it was the teacher's turn, she would close her eyes reverently. "I'm thankful for my eyes to see," she would intone. "I'm thankful for my ears to hear. I am thankful for my legs to walk, my mind to think, my fingers to touch." At the time, we were all in agreement that Miss S. was out of her mind. But now that I'm older, and a bit more worn, I wake up each morning thankful for what vision and hearing I have left, for a mind that is intact and for the fact that I can still walk miles with pleasure. Not only am I thankful for these wonders, but I never fail to express them at every opportunity. I finally have come to understand what she meant.

Years ago, I had a Buddhist teacher in Thailand who would remind all of his students that there was always something to be thankful for. He'd say, "Let's rise and be thankful, for if we didn't learn a lot today, at least we may have learned a little. And if we didn't learn even a little, at least we didn't get sick. And if we did get sick, at least we didn't die. So let us all be thankful."

A man's indebtedness. . . is not a virtue; his repayment is.
Virtue begins when he dedicated himself
actively to the job of gratitude.
RUTH BENEDICT

Analyzing love

I wonder why it seems so important these days to analyze everything. Someone says, "I love you," and we feel we should question what they mean. We want to know what they are really saying and wonder what they are really feeling. We spend endless hours dissecting why someone would say this or do that, putting under a microscope things that would be better simply accepted.

It is certainly true that the more we know about something or someone, the more we can understand them. But we can never know everything about anything and that's alright too. There is a certain magic in the fact that even after a lifetime of relating the deepest feelings, thoughts and actions may remain incomprehensible.

What we need to know about loving is no great mystery. We all know what constitutes loving behavior; we need but act upon it, not continually question it. Overanalysis often confuses the issue and in the end brings us no closer to insight. We sometimes become too busy classifying, separating, and examining, to remember that love is easy. It's we who make it complicated.

A man lives by believing something, not by
debating and arguing about many things.
THOMAS CARLYLE

Expressing needs

No one was ever meant to cry or suffer alone. Yet there are many among us who will go for years suffering in silence rather than ask for the help we need so badly. We believe that others should be cognizant of our pain, even though we say nothing about it.

It is from emotional strength, not weakness, that we are able to solicit help. Fear of rejection or of ridicule or of whatever we contrive to keep our pain hidden, will have to be overcome or we will never receive the support we require.

In asking for help we are, actually, paying a compliment. We are suggesting to another that we trust them to help us during a time of great vulnerability. We do not expect solutions from them. We ask only that they be present, that they give us the temporary support we require while we find our own solutions.

A healthy "I need you," is an important expression of love.

I believe the first test of a truly great man is humility.
JOHN RUSKIN

Learning patience

Patience is not a highly cultivated trait in our culture. We even find ourselves becoming impatient with patience. We want to have action and answers now. We want to change our lives now. We want fame now. We overlook the fact that if we want right action, correct answers and permanent change, we often must wait. Things such as careful analysis, thoughtful consideration, and quiet deliberation take time.

This is especially true in love. We want the perfect lovers in the ideal relationships and we want them now. If the hoped-for-relationship doesn't happen instantaneously, we head for the exit, disregarding the time, endurance and steadiness so integral to the process. Patience implies the willingness to bear suffering, endure delay and persevere when things become difficult. Its reward is in strengthened commitments and patience returned. Patience is the basic quality of which forever-aftering is made.

Anything worthwhile is worth waiting for.
ANONYMOUS

What we think and believe is what we are

Someone I've known well for years lives always just this side of breakdown. She is convinced that the world is a cruel and pitiless place and that tragedy is lurking just ahead, ready to pounce on her in an instant if she should allow herself to be off guard.

She is certain that if she plans a picnic, it will rain; if the phone rings, it will be someone with dreadful news; a telegram is sure to be a death announcement. People, she will tell you at the drop of a phrase, are either ignorant, hypocritical, treacherous, or all of these. Of course she sees me, the eternal optimist, as naive, fatuous and not to be believed.

Like a self-fulfilling prophecy, her dismal view of life, her low opinion of people and her expectation of doom are too often confirmed. I don't think she could survive otherwise.

Love is not foolish. It recognizes the dark side of life. But for its own survival, it doesn't make negativity a permanent abode.

If you keep saying that things are going to be bad,
you have a chance of being a prophet.
ISAAC SINGER

Trivia is the pestilence that eventually kills love

It is rarely the big things that interfere with the growth of love. Rather it is the small, seemingly insignificant things that are the most defeating. She likes to squeeze the toothpaste tube in the middle; he likes it neat and squeezes it from the bottom. Though this is cause for some annoyance, neither is willing to see it as any real threat to their relationship.

He likes to toss his clothes over a chair when he gets home from work; she prefers he hang them up, keeping things tidy. She likes routine, going out on specific nights of the week, having guests on weekends only; he likes spontaneity, going out when the spirit moves him, he welcomes guests any night of the week. He likes to go to the same place every year for their vacation; she likes change, wants to see new places and have different adventures.

None of these differences in themselves are grounds for ending a relationship, but it is interesting to note how they are magnified and intensified until they end up becoming the irreconcilable differences.

It's also interesting how two people can readily join forces to overcome a major crisis in their lives, yet be overwhelmed by some little, insignificant thing that has been allowed to grow and fester.

It is wise to do a house cleaning of trivia every now and then by facing the pet peeves that become fiery dragons before we know it.

*We can offer up much in the large, but making sacrifices in little
things is what we are seldom equal to.*
JOHANN WOLFGANG VON GOETHE

Loneliness as a source of love

It is well to remember that no matter how many people love us, surround us, or are concerned for our welfare, in a very real sense, we are alone. No one, no matter how caring, can ever truly understand us, our fears, our hopes, our dreams. We are strangers even to ourselves and many of us spend our lifetimes trying to understand who we really are.

This estrangement can be the source of great loneliness, but it need not be. In reality, it offers a way of confronting our fears through self-revelation. We will only know who we are when we are willing to dig deeply into the inner recesses of our selves. Others will only know who we are when we are willing to risk in self-disclosure. The task is arduous, frightening and ongoing.

Through the acceptance of our aloneness, we can begin to glimpse the true worth of love and why we can't live without it.

Loneliness and the feeling of being unwanted
is the most terrible poverty.
MOTHER TERESA

Love has acquired its
tenuous reputation
because it has, for
so long, been left
in the hands of
amateurs.

Adaptability in love

One of the most basic tenets of science is that adaptability is the key to survival. This is no less basic to loving in that we are often required to subordinate our immediate desires to the needs of those we love. Their well-being and contentment must be as important to us as our own, perhaps more so.

Individuals unwilling to adapt or modify their behaviors look upon compromise as psychological weakness, at best a dreaded consequence. They fail to understand that there is a great difference between yielding through coercion and yielding willingly. Giving in is an important kind of giving when people love each other. What we think we may have lost in terms of one-upmanship or control, we have gained tenfold in terms of security and peaceful coexistence. You don't lose in compromise, you find.

A great deal of good can be done in the world
if one is not too careful who gets the credit.
A JESUIT MOTTO

Choice

Those who suffer the illusion that they are nothing more than human computers, manipulated by programmers over which they have no control, will never fully know love or live life.

We are born having no like or equal. Our mind, character and spirit are distinctly our own. As we develop these qualities, we may sometimes find ourselves at the mercy of ruthless, thoughtless individuals who would desire to make us their clones. But as long as we believe that we are free to make choices, we are safe. This great power, to choose rather than always to be chosen, remains ours forever.

Still, there will always be people to tell us that we are powerless and pawn-like. To accept or reject the truth of this is just another choice we have.

There are too many successful examples not to believe that we are free to alter who we are, what we believe, and what we see as our purpose and goals. We can choose to love or hate, be happy or despairing, be free or oppressed, forgiving or bitter. Having freedom includes taking responsibility for choices made. In the long run, we are responsible for our lives and how we live them.

I discovered I always have choices
and sometimes it's only a choice of attitude.
JUDITH M. KNOWLTON

The only time we fail at love is when we blame our failure on others

We are not born perfect lovers, so few of us will escape making loving fools of ourselves. Love is always there, to be learned and to be improved upon. If we are willing to acknowledge our mistakes and accept our failures, we can see them as catalysts for change rather than reasons for retreat.

As soon as we place the blame for our failure upon someone else, we limit our opportunities for growth. (Who needs to improve when it is always "their" fault?) Such an attitude is always self-defeating.

If we find ourselves unloved and unloving, the fault is ours. There can be no such thing as failing in love. We can fail to love or fail love, but we don't fail in love until we place the blame for our failure on someone else.

When a man blames others for his failures,
it is a good idea to credit others with his successes.
HOWARD W. NEWTON

The real challenge of love is to maintain our personal dignity without intruding on that of others

Our most valuable possession is our personal dignity. When we lose that, we have nothing. Since we all have value and are different from each other, it is ludicrous to measure one person's worth against another's. People who evaluate worth in others by their monetary value, their work, or by what lifestyle they choose, call into question their own intelligence and sensitivity.

If we are all equal in the eyes of God, who can put themselves up as a higher judge? We only become entrapped in this losing scenario when we allow others to be determiners of our worth. As long as we believe in ourselves, maintain our self-respect, pride and sense of humor, we are safe from such intruders.

When we belittle in order to aggrandize ourselves, it is a sign of our own weakness. We become more worthy of compassion than contempt, for, in reality, we are revealing our desperate need to be loved.

To behave with dignity is nothing more than
to allow others freely to be themselves.
SOL CHANELES

It is only when we
have experienced love
that we truly realize
what would be lost
by missing it.

Stop questioning, just love, and you will have solved its mystery

With something as complex and all consuming as love, it is not unexpected that we should choose to move judiciously. This is especially understandable when we feel that love has somehow wronged us. Ego wounds heal slowly, the more so when we take defeat and failure as a sign that we are unlovable. To continually analyze everything and everyone we associate with love prevents us from making sound judgments. Eventually it immobilizes us. Why and who and how we love does not benefit from microscopic scrutiny.

A reader wrote to tell me of her problem with falling in love. The more time she spent analyzing and anticipating the possible course of the relationship in question, the more impossible it became for her to make a decision. "Perhaps," she concluded, "I should just stop questioning and just love into the answers." Perhaps.

Not to decide is to decide.
HARVEY COX

Losing

One of the fundamental aspects of loving is the willingness to unite deeply with another person. It is natural that we should desire to be a deep and integral part of those we love. We believe that we can only bring them happiness if we can know them mind, body and spirit.

There is an inherent danger in this when we become so thoroughly involved with another that we lose ourselves. In so doing, we become less to everyone who loves us. For to totally merge our identity with another is to deny our past and all that makes us who we are. A loving relationship works better as a voluntary coming together of two separate individuals. Through their dedication and respect for each other, they create a new entity, which is neither one of them, but part of both—their relationship.

New relationships are always fragile; those that survive seem either to age gracefully or end up simply aging. The difference it seems, is in two people who have maintained their personal integrity and who have also been willing to merge their efforts and uniqueness into shaping their love.

We will find it necessary to relinquish something of ourselves with each new relationship, but it is wise to be forever cautious not to totally lose ourselves in the process.

There is abundant testimony that if we choose love
rather than self, we gain immeasurably.
CHARLES FIELD

You are never defeated in love until you imagine you fully understand it

Don't be taken in. There are no experts in love. I have been studying it for over twenty-five years and I am still hesitant even to define it. With each year that I live and struggle with the concept, I find new intriguing facets which keep me from ever being complacent as a lover. Those who demand to see the whole picture or the bottom line will surely remain forever frustrated. It's not so important that we receive definitive answers in love, it's that we continue to search. It would be a tragedy to reach the point of death without understanding all we can about love, for I feel certain that our lives will be defined, in the final analysis, by the love we've experienced.

To continue to grow in love is a joyous and mystical journey, full of new insight, excitement and surprise. The eventual payoff, though it may not offer us all of the answers, is well worth the trip.

The brontosaurus became extinct, but it wasn't their fault.
In order to survive, man has to evolve.
JONAS SALK

Self-sacrifice

Sacrifice for personal gain is demeaning and unnatural. But, illuminated by love, self-sacrifice becomes sacred.

Too often we have heard, "After all I have given you, this is the way you show your gratitude?" This, and so many other familiar, pitiful manipulations are degrading to any concept of love. They imply a bartering by placing conditions and expectations upon us to repay in kind.

When we give up something for someone we love, no matter how great the sacrifice, there can be no conditions. What we do, we do because we will it, free of implications of future payment, or debt, or guilt. Only in this way is sacrifice a healthy manifestation of love.

*Love that asketh love again, finds the barter naught but pain. Love
that giveth in full store, aye receives as much and more.*
DINAH MULOCK CRAIK

Love makes us more

Love encourages us to venture into places in our minds and hearts never before explored and which would never have been disclosed except for love. In essence, love reveals us to ourselves.

In love we find the security which encourages us to risk, to try again, to find new behavioral alternatives for old ways. We more deeply discover ourselves as we discover each other. From lovers we are presented with a new vision, a realization that the world we have defined for ourselves may have been delimiting and we are encouraged to open up to new perceptions made possible only through someone else's vision.

Love offers us the most fertile soil for growth. We nurture that soil by enriching it with a willingness to give up our old self and our useless preconceptions. In return, we are presented with a broader vision of ourselves and a world of limitless possibilities for our discovery. Love is not blind. It has perfect vision. It makes it possible for us to see as we have never seen before.

There is the same difference in a person before and after he is in love, as there is in an unlighted lamp and one that is burning. The lamp was there and was a good lamp, but now it is shedding light too (and this is its real function).
VINCENT VAN GOGH

We are only prepared to give and receive the love we know

Working with emotionally disturbed children over the years has served to offer me great insight. Most of these children had only experienced perversions of love. It was not surprising, then, that expressions of love terrorized them. Signs of affection were rejected and misinterpreted. Tenderness repelled them. The long road to trust had to be paved with months and years of consistent and persistent reassurance.

What they had learned to fear could finally, with time and understanding, be accepted as soothing; what they had experienced as agitating now seemed comforting; what they had perceived as detestable could now be accepted as reassuring.

The love we have to give will be contingent upon the love we have experienced. But there is hope. Love is learned through loving.

There is no harvest for the heart alone.
The seed of love must be eternally resown.
ANNE MORROW LINDBERGH

Worry never robs
tomorrow of its
sorrow, it only saps
today of its joy.

A day spent without having completed an act of love is a day lost

We all have so many possible occasions for loving and yet there is so little demonstrated love in the world. People are dying alone, crying alone. Children are being abused and elderly people are spending their final days without tenderness and love. In a world where there is such an obvious need for demonstrated love, it is well to realize the enormous power we do have to help and to heal people in our lives with nothing more complicated than an outstretched hand or a warm hug. Teresa of Avila entreated us to "accustom yourself to make many acts of love, for they enkindle and melt the soul."

Day's end is a good time to reflect on what we have done to make the world a better, more caring and loving place. If nothing springs to mind night after night, this can also be an excellent time for us to consider how we can change the world for the better. We need not perform monumental acts, but act on the simple things which are readily accomplished: that phone call we have not made, that note we have put off writing, that kindness we have failed to acknowledge. When it comes to giving love, the opportunities are unlimited and we are all gifted.

Love is not only something you feel. It is something you do.
DAVID WILKERSON

Avoiding ourselves

Most of us never get closer than three feet from ourselves. We have no real interest in who we are or why we behave as we do. We don't trust our feelings, thoughts or our dreams. We are fearful that if we were to examine ourselves closely, we would discover a Pandora's Box of horrors.

It is only when we face our suspected demons that we become able to deal with them. Though we have heard the incessant cries of philosophers and psychologists to "know thyself," it seems only vaguely relevant, so we continue to live with a stranger. How, then, can we expect to take on responsibilities for others when we have not yet come to grips with ourselves?

We cannot hide who we are and ask other strangers, hiding who they are, to love us and expect to find happiness.

The first step to knowledge is to know that we are ignorant.
LORD DAVID CECIL

Extremes of emotion distort love

When we encounter our first love, we are usually overwhelmed. We see what we want to see, rather than what there is. We do not understand when others are not astounded by the beauty, warmth, strength and brilliance of our loved one. It is like the fabled magical glasses which, when worn, were capable of creating a paradise out of hell. Reality, it would seem, casts an unendurable glare.

Emotional extremes that distort our perception of reality are capable of making fools of us all. These states are usually transitory and are rarely conducive to sound judgment. If we are willing to wait, however, we learn a sense of balance. Passions are ripened rather than inflamed; adoration is tempered with moderation. This is not to say that we lose our fire or become emotionally limp. It is only a reminder that we need to remove the emotional blinders so that we can trust our vision.

A man must see before he can say.
HENRY DAVID THOREAU

Love has greater purpose than to simply make us comfortable

Many of us seem content being passive witnesses to love, convinced that since we were born for love, it should present no problems. As soon as love brings discomfort or appears to make demands of us, our instinct is to withdraw, convinced that we were not meant to struggle.

No one said love was easy. It is a constant search replete with its share of confusion, frustration and despair. If it is comfort we seek, we might best center solely upon ourselves where we can be master, hindered neither by conflict nor the need to compromise. But as long as we bring others into our lives, we can be assured of a certain degree of conflict.

But love suffers its own kind of degradation when it becomes nothing more than a comfort zone. It is always more than just a way for two people's minimal needs to be met.

Nothing will ever be attempted if all possible
objections must first be overcome.
SAMUEL JOHNSON

The tools to make love work

Most of us have little knowledge of the tools which make love work. We shouldn't blame ourselves for this since love is mainly learned through modeling, and there are pitifully few good models. But it is reassuring to know that the tools for becoming better lovers are readily available and that it is never too late.

Actually, it's rather simple. To start with, we might ask ourselves what things give us our greatest happiness. Then we must give those things to the ones we love. It's a wonderful and simple way to start. And since everyone requires basically the same things for happiness, we can hardly ever go wrong.

When we give of what we have, we are ready to
receive what we really need.
DOUGLAS M. LAWSON

Love can be nurtured by solitude

A friend explained that his relationship was destroyed because his girlfriend wanted them to be together all the time, night and day. Any sign of his wanting to be alone was to her an indication that their relationship was in danger. "I needed my private time," he confided. "It had nothing to do with her, but she still saw it as a rejection. It became even more of a problem when I attempted to see old friends or make new acquaintances. She saw this as time stolen from her. I hope she finds that special man who will want to be inseparable. It wasn't me."

To be sure, one of the signs of real love is that we never seem to get enough of each other, and nothing seems quite as wonderful as when we are sharing it together. But no matter how much we care for someone, we should always find some time apart from them. We must have time to grow separately if we care about growing together.

Love one another, but make no bond of love; Let it rather be a moving sea between the shores of your souls. Fill each other's cup, but drink not from one cup. Give one another of your bread, but eat not from the same loaf. Sing and dance together and be joyous, but let each one of you be alone.
KAHLIL GIBRAN

Relating

Two strangers meet. Both have separate histories. Both have unique perceptions of the world. They have each learned special techniques to deal with their fears and frustrations. They come to the meeting with severe limitations as well as limitless possibilities. Their love will succeed to the extent that they are willing and able to explain themselves to each other. This should be easy, since, in loving someone, we are afforded the safety and comfort necessary for revelation. To the extent that we are willing to do this, we discover the most natural path through the destructiveness of pretense and complication.

Whether or not interplanetary communications ever
materialize, an even more grandiose project awaits us.
This is the need for human beings to communicate
with one another, here and now.
NORMAN COUSINS

Lovers forgive themselves

If you're like me, you may forget your own telephone number, but have an unfailing memory for past mistakes you've made. We compound this when we allow these memories to cloud the present, even years after they've occurred.

There are parents, for instance, who burden themselves with a lifetime of guilt for the mistakes they feel they made in bringing up their children. There are those who have made poor life decisions in work, social and personal situations and have pounded their chests raw with contrition.

Continuing to punish ourselves so far out of proportion to the wrongs we may have done is an intriguing phenomenon. It suggests that we are our own harshest judge and chief tormentor. At one time or another, we will all need the forgiveness of others, but equally important is the forgiveness we owe to ourselves. Isn't it time to liberate ourselves from our self-imposed cells of guilt and regret? Love is not about opening old wounds. It is about healing them. It is about getting up and moving forward, and getting on with life.

One forgives to the degree that one loves.
LA ROCHEFAUCOULD

Forgiveness is made easy when we can identify with others and admit to our own imperfections and an equal capacity for wrongdoing.

*A*ttempting to change
the unchangeable

It is wisely said that the only thing we have the consistent power to change is ourselves. We are free to alter how we view the world, how we respond to situations, how we react to people, what we believe and what we do. It is when we set out to change *other* people that we encounter frustration and disappointment.

If we want others to change, the best thing we can do is set a gourmet table of alternatives and invite them to partake of as many possibilities as we can offer, allowing them the prerogative to accept or reject, without judgment. Anything less than this is courting tragedy.

It is the nature of man as he grows older, to protest against changes, particularly change for the better.
JOHN STEINBECK

A well-known formula for helping love to grow

It has been said, and I am certain it's true, that there is one sure way to keep love alive: find something nice to do for, or say to, the one you love, then repeat it twenty times.

Our love must not be a thing of words and fine talk.
It must be a thing of action and sincerity.
1 JOHN 3:18

Love profits from a sense of humor

We have become too serious about everything, too tense, too stressed. We equate maturity with seriousness, and believe that wisdom comes to us only through sober reflection and long considered judgments.

I was at a dinner party once where the conversation went from one morose discussion to another. Illness, crime, neurosis, the failing economy, our periled environment: it was unrelenting. All at once, an elderly man leapt up from the table and shouted, "Play time!" Of course, everyone thought he had gone completely mad. Too many at the table had learned to stifle play and had forgotten the value of mad impulses.

Most of us seem to prefer a predictable life, quiet and free from excesses. Few would choose a passionate existence, unforetellable and turbulent. I wonder what happened to the fun-loving spirits we once were, the wonder we allowed to dominate our days? When did gathering with friends become occasions solely for sounding the bell of doom? Our straight laces do, indeed, need some serious loosening from time to time, for our own sake and for the sake of those who love us. The weight of the world is a terrible thing to be saddled with. We should refuse to carry it if it is at the expense of the lighter load of laughter and lightheartedness.

The most useless day is that in which we have not laughed.
CHARLES FIELD

Love what you love with a passion

Love is an emotion of extremes. It challenges our patience, our understanding and our resources. It heightens our perceptions, and increases our energy and vitality. It is not for the easily defeated or the quickly disillusioned.

If we are determined to be lovers, we shall have to accept and acknowledge our passions. Of course we risk being led into mysterious, uncharted, hazardous places, but we can be assured that our lives will never be dull.

The best way to know God is to love many things.
VINCENT VAN GOGH

Coping

It appears, at times, that some people get all the breaks. While they climb the ladder to happiness and success, we seem stuck on the first rung. It seldom occurs to us that those who succeed are those who are accepting of life's problems. It is good to know that no life is trouble free, that much of what happens to us is unavoidable, and that we cannot always be in control.

This is not to say that we should spend our lives putting up with things. I cannot accept the idea that life is something to be endured.

Learning to cope is a *skill* for life, not a *way* of life. Living fully *is* a way of life, with loving fully as its most perfect complement.

Expect trouble as an inevitable part of life and when it comes, hold your head high, look it squarely in the eye and say, "I will be bigger than you. You cannot defeat me."
ANN LANDERS

Love creates an "us" without destroying a "me"

Maintaining control in a relationship seems to be a driving concern in some individuals. With fiendish gusto they actively seek out individuals, who, for the sake of getting along, allow themselves to be dominated. Their need to assert their autonomy gives way to the path of least resistance. Whether they are too uncertain of themselves or just too weak to resist, they relinquish their individuality.

The tragedy here is that the more we allow others to exercise power over us, the more we lose touch with who we are and what we have a right to expect. Once lost, the struggle to regain our person is an uphill one at best, especially when we convince ourselves that it is our lot in life to be submissive to the will of another. No one is given life to willingly relinquish it on command. To do so in the name of love is a complete distortion of the word.

Most of us are taught from an early age to pay far more attention to signals coming from other people than from within. We are encouraged to ignore our own needs and wants and to concentrate on living up to others' expectations.
NATHANIEL BRANDON

Love isn't the problem, we are

When I hear someone sigh, "Loving is so difficult," I'm tempted to ask, "Compared to what?" The conflicts we encounter in loving are often simply opportunities which ask for a little extra effort on our part. Perhaps we need to see innocence in another's transgressions, and not be so critical of them. Perhaps we need to be silent and listen more often with our hearts. We may find it better making allowances than making points. Perhaps we'd be wiser to overlook weaknesses rather than playing on them.

No one ever said that love was easy. But in the last analysis, it is not the problems that love brings to us, but rather what we bring to love that really matters.

It is sad not to be loved,
but it is much sadder not to be able to love.
MIGUEL DE UNAMUNO

On this earth there is
no perfect love,
only human love.

Love has no room for jealousy

We should never subscribe to the idea that we are only *truly* loved when we are loved exclusively. To the contrary, we are all capable of loving any number of people at the same time—lovers, family and friends. A person who can care only for a single individual usually has a problem with caring in general. Love is not a quality that is diluted when given freely and often. Rather, it is enriched and intensified.

To require that someone exist for us alone is an egocentric illusion which should have been left behind in childhood. It is demeaning to be regarded as a thing which can be possessed and controlled.

If we are so insecure in our relationships that they must be constantly protected and guarded, it might be well to call up that little child within us and help him or her to grow up. Absolute control over another person is neither possible, desirable nor loving. Instead it destroys what it sets out to protect.

The bird of paradise alights
only upon the hand that does not grasp.
JOHN BERRY

142

*L*ove survives in empathy

Empathy is understanding the other person's point of view. The Judeo-Christian Golden Rule of treating others as you would like to be treated is an example of empathy. It is a powerful human trait for strengthening our personal relations.

Empathy does not mean that we must accept the other's view. It simply means that we are willing to attempt to understand it. We will never be able to do this until we accept that everyone is composed of their own experiences, which are valid for them, even if they are at odds with ours. We cannot expect that everyone will perceive the world in the same way we do. We will truly have empathy when we can step outside of ourselves and attempt to see how things look to other people.

Many times I have met disagreeable individuals who, on face value, might have been easily dismissed and forgotten. When I took the time, however, to learn more about them, I almost always emerged with more acceptance of their behavior. It has taught me to withhold negative snap judgments knowing how wrong they can often be.

When empathy becomes a habit, and we are no longer ruled by the passion of the moment, our ability to love will be boundless.

When you look for the good in others,
you discover the best in yourself.
MARTIN WALSH

*O*ur hearts have a mind of their own

The heart is the place where we live our passions. It is frail and easily broken, but wonderfully resilient. There is no point in trying to deceive the heart. It depends upon our honesty for its survival.

Often, when we suspect that our hearts may break, we retreat to our own safe havens where we have learned to mask our pain or deny it altogether. There we pretend to be safe and secure.

Struggling with pains of the heart is essential for positive change. Few things of lasting value happen without some conflict. If there is nothing to oppose us, we move from action to complacency, where eventually we discover that the absence of pain is not necessarily the best answer.

Some people feel with their heads and think with their hearts.
G.C. LICHTENBERG

I will love you if...

There is an often heard refrain among lovers. I call it the "I will love you if" message. This is love offered with specified conditions and it simply doesn't work. It suggests a bartering or a using of love, or the threat of losing it, as a continual possibility.

"I will love you if you stay home and take care of the house."

"I will love you if you are successful."

"I will love you if you agree with me."

"I will love you if you stay constantly at my side."

And on and on.

It's always difficult to meet these expectations, but they become even more perplexing when love is being used as leverage. Love should be a given, a constant. The message must be, "I will love you, no matter. Don't worry about losing my love."

Attempting to redesign another human being is fraught with danger, especially when we threaten to withhold our love as a means of accomplishing it.

No human creature can give orders to love.
GEORGE SAND

Love and the question of planning ahead

If love and life were more predictable, we'd surely have fewer problems, but they'd all be replaced by an unrelenting boredom. We can rejoice, then, that our world is as unprescribed as it is.

We actually know very little about what is going to happen in the next moment. Planning ahead may give us a certain security, but it also has a decided ring of futility to it considering how uncertain everything is.

I have a dear friend whose marriage was considered ideal by those who knew her. One day her husband left for work at his usual hour, after his favorite breakfast and the habitual loving embrace of parting. But he never came back. About midday, my friend got a call from the Los Angeles County Morgue requesting that she come and identify her husband who had been killed in an auto accident. Years of planning dissolved in one brief phone call.

As long as we have life, it will continue to unfold unpredictably. We are wise to go with it, secure in the knowledge that the present moment is ours and be content to let the future tell its own story.

In the face of an obstacle which is impossible
to overcome, stubbornness is stupid.
SIMONE DE BEAUVOIR

Love and the frail vision of self

Psychologists and linguists tell us that before we are young adults it is likely that we will have heard such negative words as "stupid," "idiot," "nuisance," "imbecile," "obnoxious," directed toward us over 15,000 times. Fifteen thousand pronouncements of our inadequacies over a period of maybe seventeen years can take its toll, even among the most confident and self-assured. It is no small wonder that many spend a lifetime dealing with feelings of inferiority.

A knowledge that words don't make it so, that we are not simply a multitude of inadequacies and faults, that others' evaluations of us may be made in ignorance, can put us on a path to developing a new, healthier, more realistic vision of ourselves from which love is certain to profit.

Words, like angels, are powers which have invisible power over us. They are personal presences which have whole mythologies , . . . ; and their own guarding, blaspheming, creating, and annihilating effects.
JAMES HILLMAN

Love is constant, it is
we who are fickle.
Love does guarantee,
people betray. Love
can always be trusted,
people cannot.

Don't miss life
while waiting for love

We often feel there is something lacking in our experience with love, but we don't know what to do about it. We only know that our bewilderment takes us in directions we don't want to go. We are not even able to identify the unshakeable, disturbing feelings we are experiencing, although they seem to be at the core of our very being. We find ourselves the unwitting pawns of the game of love, a game we don't understand.

The solution to this dilemma is usually found in action. We need to actively engage in living life with a greater determination than ever before, seeking solutions as much as avoiding the emptiness. We need to show more tenderness, reveal more patience, be more forgiving, and express more gratitude for the things we *do* have. Positive action has a way of reopening the heart.

There is nothing wrong with waiting for love as long as we continue living fully in the process.

Time is nature's way of keeping
everything from happening at once.
ANONYMOUS

You can love others only as much as you love yourself

Most religions of the world command that we love ourselves. The essence of the mandate is that we must be aware of the inherent harmony that exists between the love we feel for others and the love we must, of necessity, feel for ourselves, if we are to love at all. While some say otherwise, self-love is a healthy necessity and as long as it is directed outward, has nothing to do with egocentricity. Self-love is founded in the fundamental truth that we are only able to give what we have and teach what we know. The goal is to develop the best possible self, enabling us to share it with others. It is impossible to love others more than we do ourselves and since our love is limitless, there is limitless hope.

The mandate to 'love your neighbor as you love yourself'
is not just a moral mandate. It's a psychological
mandate. Caring is biological. One thing you get from
caring for others is you're not lonely. And the more
connected you are to life the healthier you are.
JAMES LYNCH

Communicating love

In 1983 I conducted a very interesting study. I asked lovers who had succeeded in staying together for many happy and productive years what they considered to be the characteristics most responsible for their success in love. More than 85 percent of the hundreds of respondents said that the most essential quality for a lasting relationship was the ability to communicate.

Communication is the art of talking *with* each other, not to each other. It is saying what we mean, what we feel, clearly, without deception or disguise. Contrary to the popular belief, it is an acquired *skill*, and not a natural byproduct of two people coming together. All things that "go without saying" or that are "understood" between two people in love can build up a mountain of miscommunication. We cannot hear what the other is not saying; and sometimes, when we finally do, it's too late.

If two people who love each other let a single instant wedge
itself between them, it grows—it becomes a month,
a year, a century; it becomes too late.
JEAN GIRAUDOUX

Love is an art as well as a science

Not long into a relationship we realize that it requires an inordinate amount of inventiveness, as well as intellectual ability, to keep it alive. The one who relaxes in the arms of love usually awakens at the feet of disillusionment. Love demands our vigilance as well as our awareness to all that is happening around us. We must be sensitive to even subtle clues which point to needs, changes, fears, frustrations. We must be ready for creative action and not allow ourselves to be restricted by preconceptions or habitual behaviors.

It's unfortunate how we take our relationships for granted. Where love is concerned, the result is often outright loss. Then, as so often happens, enormous effort is expended to regain what was lost simply because what was already ours had not been properly maintained.

Creative thinking may mean simply the realization that
there's no particular virtue in doing things
the way they have always been done.
RUDOLF FLESCH

Believing enough to forgive

Trust is based on faith. When we entrust our hearts to someone else, we assume that they will never deliberately attempt to hurt or abuse us. We'd like to count on the people we love to be honest, reliable and just. We'd like to think that they will be responsible, but sadly, this is not always true. Since we are all imperfect and vulnerable, we may find ourselves deceiving or being deceived. It is at these times that we must call upon our ability to forgive, from which wounds heal and faith is restored.

Trusting implies forgetting the past and moving forward, or just trying again, always with the knowledge that the effort, however imperfect, is worth it. Our goal, after all, is humanness, not godliness.

The truth is more important than the facts.
FRANK LLOYD WRIGHT

Love is enriched by play

Too often we relegate playing to childhood. Adult games are usually structured, have defined rules and are played to win. Children play just for the joy of it.

Lovers who play together know the value of fun, laughter and surprise. When they indulge in make-believe, they find it opens areas of imagination that are often lost in the routine that most relationships fall into. Creative play can help us relate to people and things in new ways. Play encourages lighthearted cooperation and gets us away from the competitiveness of our society. There is no striving to win when we are playing for fun.

I once suggested to a couple that they play more. They welcomed the idea, in light of the pressures they were feeling in their lives. So they bought a ping-pong table. Each night after work they played. But what started out as fun quickly became a nightly battle. He began to talk about "showing no mercy" and she expressed her need to "smash the ball down his throat." Happily they opted for less competitive play before a friendly little game of ping-pong undermined their marriage. They now use the table to sort laundry.

O. Fred Donaldson suggested that "play is an act of insurrection in a dehumanized world." And it is surely true. The sole purpose of play is to have fun, to be diverted and amused, to frolic meaninglessly and gleefully for a while, outside the realm of the intellect. When we do this, we discover a positive side of ourselves that celebrates life without analysis, one of the basic components of love.

> *Now it is characteristic of play that*
> *one plays without reason and there must*
> *be no reason for it. Play is its own good reason.*
> *LIN YUTANG*

When love is true, it is selfless

Time and again examples of loving individuals are found who ceased looking for love and began to practice it in selfless action. I am not suggesting that we can all emulate Mother Teresa, Victor Frankl, or Dag Hammersköld, only that we learn from their works that the highest form of love comes from transcending the self and focusing on the needs of others and the world we live in.

It is a strange paradox that in forgetting the self, we see ourselves more clearly; in the giving of self, we receive the greatest benefit.

After a very serious heart operation and severe complications, I began to recover when I found that I had the power to bring feelings of courage, peace and joy to the other patients in the ward. I soon forgot *my* needs in fulfilling theirs.

When we love someone, their joy, growth and welfare become paramount. Our joy comes from being the vessel for their fulfillment.

Only to the extent that someone is living out this self transcendence of human existence, is he truly human or does he become his true self. He becomes so, not by concerning himself with his self's actualization, but by forgetting himself and giving himself, overlooking himself and focusing outward.
VICTOR E. FRANKL

Love is not about
opening old
wounds, it's about
healing them.

Happiness in love

Happiness is difficult to define. It's a very personal thing. For some it comes rarely and is only brought on by extraordinary circumstances. I, on the other hand, am most happy with ordinary things: a dinner with friends, a walk in a park, a good conversation, a hug. Since each of us is unique, what makes one person happy may have the opposite effect upon another.

Happiness in love is more than just ease and comfort. It will not be found in the pursuit of momentary pleasures, nor will it come from accepting someone else's definition of it. The happiness that lovers find in each other is created by them through patient and deliberate effort.

Love is so often portrayed as an intoxicant, having the power to mislead and momentarily seduce us. Much is advertised, but little is offered in the way of lasting pleasures. This will always be so as long as happiness is viewed as nothing more than a passing experience. If we desire that our happiness be more than an irregular and transitory feeling, then we will be required to bring to it a sound and strong commitment and make our own happiness.

Knowing that we are in a position to conjure up and shape our own happiness is precious knowledge. From there we can learn to bring into our lives the things that make us happy and keep them there, rather than waiting for irregular visits.

*We tend to forget that happiness doesn't come as a result
of getting something we don't have, but rather of recognizing
and appreciating what we do have.*
FREDERICK KOENIG

When love gets in a rut

In most relationships there will be times when we feel trapped and we wonder why. It is not only our happiness, but our sanity as well that we feel we need to preserve.

Our first responses are to look elsewhere or to run, anything but face the music. It's much easier to complain about our condition than to actually do something about it. Though the complaining may help us to feel better for a while, it never improves anything.

The first step in getting out of a rut is to stop spinning your wheels and start thinking about what you want to do about it. *Doing* something does not include increasing the volume of your complaints.

Too often we run from the very thing we need the most and as a result, find ourselves alone, unhappy and lonely. There is a better way and it lies in growth.

The reason why worry kills more people than work
is that more people worry than work.
ROBERT FROST

When one
discovers that most of us
are mad, love stands explained

Loving behavior doesn't stand close scrutiny. It often defies logical explanation and rational discussion. There are few things about it, in fact, that can be predicted, so we are left to puzzle over each and every instance of love as a unique phenomenon.

The years have convinced me that there is a streak of madness in even the most sane among us and that if we don't act upon this madness in the fanciful sense, we will surely go mad, in the classical sense.

How else but in a setting of madness can love ever be explained? Why else would someone be willing to embrace for life another person who in most ways is still a stranger? How do we continue to love our children when they accuse us of being dull and meddling and make conscious efforts to avoid us? Why do we allow ourselves to become emotional wrecks, almost unable to function, over a tragic love affair, merely to seek out another even before we've regained our senses? How can we be willing to submerge our egos for love of another? Surely the only answer is that we must be mad. Accepting this, as I have little difficulty doing, makes love life's most wonderful, invigorating experience.

He dares to be a fool, and that is the first
step in the direction of wisdom.
JAMES GIBBONS HUNEKER

Perfection is not a requirement to love, but honesty is

Most of us lie to ourselves and others, believing that in so doing, we make our world simpler and more comfortable. But over time, lies, however small, create rather than solve problems. Most lies in love come from the false belief that we have to be perfect to be loved. We fear the truth for the weaknesses it may expose in us. We need to be reminded that excellence is the *pursuit* of perfection, not its achievement.

We lie to others because we feel that we must be loved by everyone. We strive to keep everyone happy all of the time. Even if this were possible, it would be depleting.

We lie to ourselves to avoid facing problems. We learn to cover over unpleasant realities through our self-deceptions. The truth is that by ignoring or hiding our problems, especially in love, they are usually compounded.

Lying does not work. It is one of the leading causes of failed relationships. Nothing can be more devastating than the realization that we have been deceived by the very people in whom we have placed our trust.

Honesty is always the best policy. There is no exception. The process begins with being honest with ourselves and ends with caring enough for others to offer them the same.

Honesty is the first chapter of the book of wisdom.
THOMAS JEFFERSON

Deep intimacy and love

There is a certain element of risk in seeking closeness with another human being. Acknowledging our need for others can be very frightening. It makes us vulnerable. The paradox is that we need to open ourselves to someone, but we want to do so without risk. We want to consign ourselves without commitment; we want closeness without vulnerability. Yet, intimacy can only come when we are willing to reach out to others without guarantee, as we hope others will do.

This need is universal, inborn. There can be no doubt that everyone feels this as deeply as we do. A desire for intimacy is a sign of strength, not weakness; maturity, not neurotic need.

When love is accompanied with deep intimacy, we rise to the highest level of human experience. In this exalted space, we willingly surrender our egos and attain a glimpse of the rapture that can be ours. Boundaries are blurred; there are no limitations. We become one and, at the same time, both.

It is not our toughness that keeps us warm at night, but our
tenderness which makes others want to keep us warm.
HAROLD LYON

Love is saying "yes" to life

Life is always an adventure, whether it is directed by love or by fear. Fear is the confining of life ... the "no."

Love is the liberating of life ... the "yes."

Say "yes!"

The fear of life is the favorite disease of the Twentieth Century.
WILLIAM LYON PHELPS

Security and loving

We cannot live by love alone, powerful though it may be.

When I was growing up in my large family, we constantly subsisted below the poverty level. Food was often scarce, space was at a premium in a house built for half our number and clothing was almost always hand-me-downs. Still, we not only survived, we thrived. I was certainly aware that there were others who had more things than we did, but the security that came from love was a powerful compensation.

We had each other. We were never lonely. We had Mama's sense of humor and culinary magic. (How she prepared wonderful meals with so little to work with, I'll never know.) We had Papa's warmth and gardening skills. (How he brought such bounty from such a small plot of land mystifies me still.)

Love was always there to help us overcome whatever lack there was. More importantly, we all gained a deep insight into what the real basic need truly was.

Keep love in your heart. A life without it is like a
sunless garden when the flowers are dead.
OSCAR WILDE

Most of us remain
strangers to
ourselves, hiding
who we are, and ask
other strangers,
hiding who they are,
to love us.

Love thrives on continual enrichment

To have a long-lasting relationship, we must avoid complacency. More love has been lost on the island of contentment than in any sea of torment.

Love demands that we keep our minds open and stimulated, which is really easier than we think. It can be accomplished in a hundred simple ways.

I know a couple who have been married over forty years and have never stopped growing. She is presently in a watercoloring class, while he is attending an income tax preparation seminar. Together they are studying Italian in anticipation of a trip to southern Italy. There is no time in their life for boredom and I have never known them to run out of something to share.

Relationships do not grow or remain stimulating without conscious effort. We must take the time to enrich our lives, and therefore our love, or we are merely coexisting. Complacency kills.

Growth is the only evidence of life.
JOHN HENRY CARDINAL NEWMAN

Hearing the sounds of love

Most of us are poor listeners if we actually listen at all. Misunderstandings because of poor listening habits have caused more unhappiness and pain than we'll ever know. The cost in loneliness, broken hearts, wasted time and injury is immeasurable.

We tend to be selective listeners, at best, hearing about half of what is said and filtering out things we deem unimportant. Even when we feel we are truly listening, we often tend to hear the wrong message. We hear what we desire or expect to hear rather than what is actually being said.

But there is hope for those of us concerned with loving communication. Listening is a learned art. Love is a perfect impetus for working at that art if for no other reason than to teach us the painful consequences of tuning people out. Concern for the feelings and well-being of others goes a long way toward changing our listening habits. We hear best what we love. Listening is love in action.

One of the best ways to persuade others is
with your ears . . . by listening to them.
DEAN RUSK

To move closer to love, we must sometimes move away from it

At times it is only by distancing ourselves, temporarily, from a seemingly hopeless situation that we can begin to engage in the acts necessary for regeneration. Stepping away from the problem provides us with time to analyze and reorganize.

It is surprising how often a solution is close at hand. Friends, counselors, family, books or workshops are good sources for discovering new alternatives. But we must be willing to take the required time to find our solutions.

When we move away from waning love for the sake of gaining new insights, we are not running from our problem, but rather moving toward possible solutions.

We cannot solve life's problems except by solving them.
M. SCOTT PECK

*L*ove compliments

I think we are usually far more generous with compliments to friends than to those we love most dearly. This happens despite the fact that behavioral scientists, and our instincts, tell us that compliments affect behavior far more powerfully than criticism. We all need to bask in the warmth and approval of someone we respect, otherwise our personal dignity becomes seriously endangered.

We have become so unaccustomed to compliments that they seem to embarrass both the giver and the receiver. We are quick to criticize, yet so guarded with praise. If the new outfit looks great, what harm can come from saying so? If the hairdo suits, why not comment? If someone is doing a good job, it can only reinforce the person to tell them so.

Praise, like love, is only meaningful when freely shared.

Vanity is so secure in the heart of man that everyone wants to be admired—even I who write this, and you who read this.
BLAISE PASCAL

Love offers no assurance

Love would be far less intimidating to some of us if it came with a guarantee. Not even the sanction of the church and the law provides one. We will always have to trust in love.

Few of us are free of the pain and tears that betrayal in love can inflict. These experiences often leave us hardened and unforgiving. Of course, we blame love for our unhappiness. We ignore the fact that love is constant. It is people who are fickle. Love does offer a guarantee, people betray. Love can be trusted, people are changeable. The only real assurance we will ever have in love comes through applying our energies to making ourselves worthy of lasting love. Then, there is nothing to fear.

Hell is not to love anymore.
GEORGE BERNANOS

Love and traumas

Most of our traumas come through loss, death, divorce, failing health, financial setback, or broken friendships. No life is ever free of such emotionally painful experiences. There is no way to avoid them. They are part of the reality of existence.

Being traumatized threatens our total equilibrium, especially when the loss is irreversible. What was once accepted as usual and predictable suddenly seems bizarre and unsettling.

It takes time to accept the irreversibility of a loss. Adjusting to a life that will never be the same can expose weaknesses within ourselves—great courage is often needed to adapt and carry on. But it can also reveal strengths and resources we never knew we had.

Still, the first and usual response to loss is to feel pity for ourselves and place blame on someone or something for our misfortune. We accuse God, society, or loved ones, anyone at hand. Actually, when we take the responsibility of overcoming our traumas, we become better acquainted with ourselves and achieve a greater acceptance of life.

A time of pain or loss of hope can be an awakening which opens us to ourselves, dispels our ignorance, and erases our false perceptions.

The only lasting trauma is the one we suffer without positive change.

In time, our pain subsides, our wounds heal and we discover an all important truth: what remains after all is the most valuable thing we possess, life itself.

Happiness is the interval between periods of unhappiness.
DON MARQUIS

The changing face of love

Since love is never experienced in the same way twice, it always confounds and challenges us. Every new love calls for unique behaviors, full use of our rational and intuitive selves.

Each new situation comes with its own complex demands. We bring our past experiences to bear upon each new love only to discover that they seem useless, compelling us to discover novel, ingenious ways to deal with them. Old habits, styles and attitudes no longer seem to serve this love's new demands. But we need never fear the changing face of love, because we only fail at love when we behave as if we know it all.

The only sense that is common in the long run,
is the sense of change . . . and we all instinctively avoid it.
E.B. WHITE

Giving in is an
important kind of
giving when people
love each other.

The power of human love

As human beings, none of us is perfect. Frailties and imperfections abound. We succumb to:
anger
impetuosity
revenge
stubbornness
conceit
irrationality
lack of compassion
lack of humility
destructiveness
mischievousness
fearfulness
pridefulness
cunning
falsehood
dishonesty
indecision
cowardliness
prejudice
hate

When we love each other in spite of these imperfections, we begin to realize the inexplicable power of love.

The truth is so simple that it is regarded as pretentious banality.
DAG HAMMERSKÖLD

*L*ove and hope

There is no medicine like hope, no tonic more powerful than the belief that every trauma has a solution. The ability to hope allows us to face the trials of daily life. It reminds us that no matter what happens, we will prevail. No one need be a hopeless victim; few situations are completely without remedy. With hope we can change a potential tragedy into an achievement. If the situation won't change, we can change to meet the situation.

For those who believe, hope does, indeed, spring eternal.

The capacity for hope is the most significant fact of life.
It provides human beings with a sense of destination
and the energy to get started.
NORMAN COUSINS

*L*ove and compassion

We are still incomplete creatures floundering in a complex, challenging world in which compassion helps to save us all. When we are compassionate, we become more realistic in our expectations, less demanding, and more flexible. We are less likely to inflict wounds, hurt feelings and indulge in recriminations. We allow for human frailty and change. Put more simply, we permit people to be who they are and to act upon what they feel, encouraging them to become more themselves.

Compassion is an act of tolerance, where kindness and forgiveness reign. When we make the compassionate choice, we enhance the dignity of each individual, which is the very essence of loving them.

But since human beings are inherently compassionate, compassion in
them can be awakened and generated; whatever their age and
however horrendous their past experiences have been.
THEODORE ISAAC RUBIN

Being who we are

People who feel good about themselves are not easily threatened by the future. They enthusiastically maintain a secure image whether everything is falling apart or going their way. They hold to a firm base of personal assuredness and self-respect that remains constant. Though they are concerned about what others think of them, it is a healthy concern. They find external forces more challenging than threatening.

Perhaps the greatest sign of maturity is to reach the point in life when we embrace ourselves—strengths and weaknesses alike—and acknowledge that we are all that we have; that we have a right to a happy and productive life and the power to change ourselves and our environment within realistic limitations. In short, we are, each of us, entitled to be who we are and become what we choose.

*Every individual has a place to fill in this world and is important
in some respect whether he chooses to be or not.*
NATHANIEL HAWTHORNE

*B*lame

Most of us are experts at blame. We've learned to lay our failures and problems conveniently at the feet of others. "I can't do anything about the way I am," a seriously troubled man said to me. "My childhood was a nightmare." Twenty years later this man's life was still on hold because of unhealed wounds. It has become apparent that the heart of his problem was not so much his troublesome past, but his compulsion to dwell on it without doing anything about it. Depression, neurosis, chronic unhappiness are not only caused by an event or a person, but also by how a person continues to respond to them.

When we realize that we are responsible for freeing ourselves from yokes of the past, we will also free everyone else of this responsibility. Only then can we begin to concentrate more on loving and less on blaming.

The man who foolishly does me wrong, I will return to him the
protection of my most ungrudging love; and the more evil
comes from him, the more good shall go from me.
BUDDHA

A simple lesson in loving

Approach everyone you meet as an individual with dignity and a life as complicated and mysterious as your own. Discard preconceptions and suspend, even for a moment, the idea that you "know this type."

Do these things and perhaps you might learn the most important lesson that love can teach us: that each person is worthy of our love simply because they are human, one of God's unique creations, and begin from there.

The measure of man's humanity is the
extent and intensity of his love for mankind.
ASHLEY MONTAGU

Love doesn't teach,
it points the way

Educators and psychologists have confirmed over the years that we learn best from modeling, by observing the behavior of those closest to us, those we admire.

For example, it has been determined that parents who want their children to read or appreciate serious music accomplish this best by being readers themselves and surrounding themselves with classical music. If they hope that their children will enjoy the pleasures of good, healthy food, they should cook and share it with them on a regular basis. By their example, they are teaching in the purest sense.

My parents were the most consummate examples of lovers I have ever known. My book, LOVE, is dedicated to them with the following statement, "To Tulio and Rosa, who didn't teach me how to love, they showed me."

Children raised in a loving environment will begin, over time, to define love in terms of what they are experiencing. The more clearly and consistently love is modeled, the more naturally and effortlessly it will become a part of their lives.

If we want to share love with someone, the most successful strategy is to be the best lover we can and let the rest take care of itself.

Every experience in life, everything with which we have come in contact in life, is a chisel which has been cutting away at our life statue, molding, modifying, shaping it. We are part of all we have met.
ORISON SWETT MARDEN

Lasting love is not a test of endurance

It is a sorry and often heard refrain that "love has vanished from our relationship." As with many such statements, this is unfair to love. It's not love that has disappeared from the relationship, we have. Lasting love is not a test of endurance. When we are able to appreciate all the things which brought us together, and deepen that appreciation over the years, we stay together. Such a relationship is one of life's great success stories.

That's the good news. The bad news for some people is that success requires effort. Healthy bonds need maintenance if they are to remain healthy; obstacles must be overcome or taken in stride. We must take into consideration the pretenses and defenses that threaten love. For our part, we should welcome the mystery, enthusiasm and challenge which will make us lovers for a lifetime.

Obstacles are those frightful things
you see when you take your eyes off the goal.
HANNAH MORE

Worry never robs tomorrow of its sorrow, it only saps today of its joy

Some of us find love and commitment a great source of pressure and/or anxiety. We worry about making the right choices. Will the relationship fail? Will we be hurt? If we expose ourselves in intimacy, will we be enough? We worry ourselves, in other words, right out of love. Love becomes a pressure, a frustration, a source of stress.

Ninety percent of what we worry about never happens. We all know this from first-hand experience. Still, we possessively hold on to our worry as if we would be frivolous to let it go. Minor problems send us into a dither, larger ones threaten to totally unravel us. We see the negative side of everything before we consider the positive (if indeed, we ever look for the positive). We have a million good reasons for worrying, since we are well versed on everything and everyone that can cause us harm.

Worry makes fools of us all. It controls our lives and leaves us with empty hearts and missed experiences. I am not suggesting that we skip merrily through life carefree and oblivious. I do suggest that we learn to sort out real concerns from the mass of imaginative and insignificant ones.

It makes no difference how deeply seated may be the trouble, how hopeless the outlook, how muddled the tangle, how great the mistake. A sufficient realization of love will dissolve it all.
EMMET FOX

We are confined in
our understanding of
other human beings
by what we know
about ourselves.

Saying "no" to love

Some of us have the mistaken notion that when we love someone we are compelled to say yes to them all the time no matter how capricious or frustrating their demands or behaviors. We feel we owe our loved ones everything in return for the love they give. In such cases it is important to understand the difference between being loved and being manipulated.

When we are led to believe that we owe something in return for someone's love, it is not love. There are times when saying no can be the greatest act of love; when being direct with our feelings can be a giant step toward greater mutual respect. Our unequivocal "no" can free us of the resentment which is inevitably an outcome of having been manipulated.

Learning that saying no may be a loving act can help us to discover resources we never knew we had, experience the dignity which comes from having been true to ourselves and acquire coping skills that will serve us forever.

Saying "no" gives meaning to our "yes."
ANONYMOUS

We have no second chance with life

Experience with death and dying has put me in touch with its inevitability and value. Death is too often feared when it is not death that is to be dreaded, but rather our willingness to apathetically accept lives unlived.

Those who deny their mortality lack the necessary driving force to face life. Existence, after all, has no meaning in and of itself. It is merely a series of moments that acquire meaning only after they have passed and are viewed in the greater tapestry of our lives. When we deliberately disregard the fact that we all shall die, that our lives are limited, we lose sight of the significance of each moment and become more willing to put them off for some future time, ignoring the reality that they are lost to us forever.

On the day we are born, we are given a life to be lived and the potential for the love to live it with. Since death comes to us mostly as a surprise, we seldom have a second chance for either.

The most compelling force for love and a life lived fully comes when we have acquired a genuine acceptance of the reality that no one has forever.

A civilization that denies death ends by denying life.
OCTAVIO PAZ

*I*n love we trust

I'm often met with cynicism because of my positive and passionate approach to trusting. I learned long ago to ignore the accusation that I am foolish and naive because of this. It continues to astound me how agitated some people get when I explain my belief that trust unites and secures as nothing else can; that without it, love cannot possibly endure. It doesn't seem to me that this is such an outrageous proposition, really, but it does seem to bring forth the detractors.

When we cease trusting, negative forces take over. Good intentions go unappreciated in minds crowded with doubt and suspicion. Expressions of love are suspected of having hidden meanings. Everyday behavior gives rise to monumental traumas. We worry that we will be deceived if we trust too much, yet do not consider the consequences of not trusting enough.

Trust men and they will be true to you; treat them
greatly and they will show themselves great.
RALPH WALDO EMERSON

Love enhances love

All loving acts directed toward us enhance our life and are essential to our well being. I accept all the love I can get. I'm not particular. The more, the better!

Sometimes the purest demonstrations of love appear through casual, spontaneous encounters, such as the stranger who stops to help us when our engine fails, or the salesperson who genuinely cares about our satisfaction. We welcome gestures like this for the simple reason that they are offered with selfless motives, with no expectations of favors returned.

While it is very human to want the love that enriches a life through a special relationship, one of the refreshing things about love is that we need never be particular where it comes from. It is important, though, that we take the time to positively acknowledge when another human being momentarily enriches our life with the touch of love. These are the reinforcements we need, the things we remember when others insist upon preaching about our loveless world and all the untrustworthy people in it.

Love is a fruit in season at all times, and
within the reach of every hand.
MOTHER TERESA

Enhancing the love that we seek

In all the world there is not a single person exactly like any of us. Everything that we produce is authentically ours. There will always be things we don't understand about ourselves as there are things we don't like about ourselves. Despite this fact, there is no good reason not to love ourselves. There is a definite dignity in our uniqueness. Our fantasies, dreams, hopes, fears, behaviors, abilities all belong only to us. They are what make us who we are and open the doors to what we can become. It is true that in our lifetime we may never really know ourselves in any complete sense, but it is our gift to God to never stop trying, for our search for love can only be enhanced through our realization of self.

To do good things in the world, first you must
know who you are and what gives meaning to your life.
PAULA P. BROWNLEE

Present love

I too often hear, "People only send me flowers when I'm sick or in the hospital, when I'm in no mood to enjoy them. I love receiving flowers and it's funny that on the day I receive the most, I won't be alive to enjoy them."

"I get presents on my birthday or at holidays, but I'd be willing to forgo some of those for a surprise gift now and then, just a sign that someone is thinking about me when they don't have to."

"I've always wanted to go to Europe, but something always seems to interfere with my plans. I guess we have to have priorities, but why is it that the things I really want to do have to be put aside for the things I have to do?"

"I meant to get him that gift he wanted. Who would ever have thought that he'd be taken from me so suddenly without my being able to give it to him?"

The only love we can utilize is that which we are experiencing in the present. It's too late for yesterday and too soon for tomorrow. Offerings and demonstrations of love cannot wait for our convenience.

Nothing is worth more than this day.
JOHANN WOLFGANG VON GOETHE

Creating fulfilling relationships

Life is so much more than settling. We often hear about people who remain in stagnant relationships, settling for a few discarded crumbs of love that may come their way, rationalizing, "that's how life is." They resign themselves to the bits of happiness that come their way as if some mystical source has predetermined and carefully measured and dispensed their allotment.

We should never be passive about our share of love and happiness. They are not things we should simply settle for. We are answerable for our love and what it does or does not bring us. If we want love in our relationships, then we are directly responsible for creating and maintaining it.

Where you find no love, put love, and you will find love.
JOHN OF THE CROSS

The best way
to come back to life
is to give it.

A life lived in love

I have a colleague who always brings a breath of fresh air into my life. She's one of those rare individuals with such a brimming passion for life that all who come to know her treasure her. She is a unique presence, dependable, but always unpredictable; wise in many ways, but with a touch of madness; always doing for others, but never forgetting her responsibility to herself; forever restless, but also quite content with her life; dedicated to maintaining close loving relationships, yet always available for some far off adventure.

I stopped wondering long ago how old my friend is. I wouldn't be surprised if she herself has lost count. I know that, more than most people, she is true to her deeply felt instincts. She refuses to waste time yearning for what could be—she's too busy doing. Her life is not filled with regrets for what might have been. She is far less concerned with what's past than with what's next.

It is her insistence on continually living life and love with a passion that energizes her and makes her ageless. If the time ever comes that she is physically unable to continue at her present pace, I believe she'll still find as many new things to do, worlds to explore and people to love. I've often thought how lucky I am to have such a friend as she, not only because of the joy she brings and the challenge she presents, but because of the shining example she represents of a life being lived so fully in love.

Every day I live I am more convinced that the waste of
life lies in the love we have not given, the powers we have not
used, the selfish prudence that will risk nothing and which,
shirking pain, misses happiness as well.
MARY CHOLMONDELEY

*E*ven love dies
with verbal neglect

Lester feels very safe in his love for Cynthia. He cares for her deeply and sincerely. He buys her gifts hoping they will convey how much she means to him, without the words he feels so awkward speaking. He often has warm, loving thoughts about her, but they go unexpressed because he feels lovingly tongue-tied. Anyway, he assumes she knows how he feels about her. As a matter of fact, most of their communications stick pretty closely to the mundane requirements of living. Lester is certain their love is unshakable and maintenance free. But one day, Cynthia announces that she wants out, she wants a divorce.

Unfortunately, Lester learned too late how utterly wrong his approach to loving and lasting relationships was. He was shocked and bewildered when this happened because he had seen himself as the perfect husband.

Love does not survive under constant verbal neglect. It eventually withers and dies. It can't be maintained by symbols and tokens, nor is it blessed by some never ending aura of forgiveness. Love must be expressed, nurtured and strengthened constantly. If we don't hear love enough, it will surely vanish.

Kindness and intelligence don't always deliver
us from pitfalls and traps. There is no way to take the
danger out of human relationships.
BARBARA GRIZZUTI HARRISON

Loving through death

A short time ago a very special friend died. We had valued and nurtured our relationship for over thirty years. We had our ups and downs during that time, but we were determined that nothing would interfere with our ever-growing friendship. I think often of the wonderful, crazy experiences we had together, of the many changes each of us went through and of the deep sharing which bonded us for life.

I know for certain that we never lose the people we love, even to death. They continue to participate in every act, thought and decision we make. Their love leaves an indelible imprint in our memories. We find comfort in knowing that our lives have been enriched by having shared their love.

Though some day we all have to part with those we love, they are not lost. We are always better for having loved. In this way, love transcends even death.

To live in the hearts we leave behind, is not to die.
THOMAS CAMPBELL

*P*redictability and love

Since human behavior is unpredictable and volatile, there can be no certitude in love. People grow, gain new insights, change directions, awaken to new needs. Changes are inevitable.

Profound as these changes may be, they are often subtle; we can be unaware of them until we are shocked that the person in whom we have invested so much of our lifetime has become a stranger. We wonder when it all happened or label it as a stage or crisis. We are not prepared to accept the idea that someone we love has changed, however imperceptibly, and we've been out of touch with it.

What is clear is that relating brings with it an element of risk and uncertainty. Those who find that disconcerting are perhaps prone to taking their love for granted. Others of us accept unpredictable behavior even in the people we know intimately. Rather than seeing it as some ominous sign of an altered personality, we can accept, even celebrate, a new and undiscovered facet of them. Anyway, predictability is a bore.

Take a chance! All life is a chance. The man who goes the furthest is generally the one who is willing to do and dare.
DALE CARNEGIE

Love is far less
concerned with
what's past than with
what's next.

Overcoming
adversity with love

Adversity requires action. Loving action brings solutions. The strength of our love is revealed in how we deal with problems and frustrations. It's easy to be pleasant and positive when all is flowing beautifully in our lives. It's when life's current changes and temporarily overpowers us that our real strength is called upon.

Love builds the best survivors. It teaches us not to waste time asking, "Why me?" but rather suggests we ask, "What now?" The first question produces needless, meaningless conflict, but the second suggests action, without the burden of self-pity and meaningless blaming. Adversity is seldom the cause of failed relationships if there is love. Rather, it is actually what helps us to change and survive.

We cannot tell what may happen to us in the strange medley of life.
But we can decide what happens in us . . . how we can take it, what
we can do with it . . . and that is what really counts in the end.
JOSEPH FORT NEWTON

Love and faith

Where there is no faith, there can be no love. Love, like faith, demands confidence without assurance. As with all things spiritual, there can be no certitude, for faith goes beyond reason and evidence, and love is above even these.

If we need them, there are many simple proofs of the existence of love in our daily lives: we plant a seed and it becomes a flower; we touch someone and they grow in strength; we wipe away tears and learn to smile again.

We begin to be comfortable with love only when, deep in our hearts, we fully accept its reality. Love hasn't a chance if we are forever questioning it or requiring it to be validated. Pascal said that, "Faith is different from proof; the latter is human, the former is from God."

It is only with the heart that one can see rightly.
What is essential is invisible to the eye.
ANTOINE DE SAINT-EXUPERY

The role of beauty in love

Though it is surely true that love brings beauty into our lives, it is also true that beauty serves to enhance our love. Each utilizes and maximizes the other.

Is there anyone so insensitive as to be completely oblivious to the beauty around us? It is so abundant, so striking even in the most mundane thing. We need only look to find it.

Beauty enlivens the commonplace. Through beauty we become more aware, our spirits are raised, our hearts are enriched, our souls are nurtured. Beauty experienced, appreciated and shared is always an expression of love.

Though we travel the world over to find the beautiful,
we must carry it with us or we find it not.
RALPH WALDO EMERSON

Making love known

An unforgettable incident occurred for me in a classroom at the University of Southern California where I taught for many years. A student in my class was diagnosed by his doctors as having muscular dystrophy which, in his case, was progressive and terminal. He was given no hope for recovery. All that he was assured of was that his last months of life would be made as painless and comfortable as possible. Though this news was devastating for him, he remained positive. He was determined to live his final days as normally as possible. Toward the end, he would come to class deeply sedated, disoriented and obviously frightened. When he realized that his class attendance was becoming impractical, he made an unusual request. He asked that each of his classmates embrace him one last time.

No sentiment, however beautifully and thoughtfully expressed, seemed to mean as much to that young man as those brief moments of tenderness. We were all reminded how very fragile our lives are and how vital it is that we make our love known, no matter our age or condition of health.

To withhold love for any reason is to deprive others of the very best we have to give. To do so for even a day diminishes a relationship. To wait a lifetime is the greatest of human tragedies.

Let him that desires to see others happy, make haste to give while his gift can be enjoyed, and remember that every moment of delay takes away something from the value of his benefaction.
SAMUEL JOHNSON

Forgiveness begins where blame ends

I was watching two children having an argument the other day. They were quarreling over some insignificant things as we often do. Their dialogue went something like this:

"You're stupid!"

"Well, so are you."

"Not as stupid as you!"

"Oh yeah? That's what you think."

After they finished this exchange, they went their separate ways. When I returned to the site not more than ten minutes later, they were playing together again, having forgotten the whole thing. No brooding, no wounded egos, no blame, no dredging up the past, no recriminations. There it was, a brief and honest exchange of angry feelings, an even briefer cooling off period, and all was forgotten.

Children are certainly much more forgiving than adults. Somewhere in the process of growing up we seem to have become experts at holding grudges, cradling fragile egos and unforgiving natures. We develop razor sharp memories of past wrongs and carry them around, ready at a moment's notice to use them as ammunition. We become skilled arguers with an unyielding sense of what is right. We are determined to win every battle and if we don't, immediately begin plotting our revenge.

Forgiveness comes only when we can identify with others and admit to our own imperfection and an equal capacity for wrongdoing.

One forgives to the degree that one loves.
LA ROCHEFAUCOULD

Being who you are is enough for love

Being ourselves in a world where everyone wants to remake us will always be our greatest challenge. The disapproval of others is a powerful deterrent, but hardly a strong enough reason to be less than who we truly are. If we want to be happy, sooner or later we will have to assert our right to be accepted as ourselves. I can't think of a more basic human right.

I am often complimented by others who say they find it refreshing that I always seem to be myself. I tell them that I attempted for years to be someone else and it didn't work.

If we desire to be treated as who and what we are, we must define who that is.

There is, in sanest hours, a consciousness, a thought that rises, independent, lifted out from all else, calm, like the stars, shining eternal. This is the thought of identity—yours for you, whoever you are, as mine for me . . . creeds, conventions, fall away and become of no account before this simple idea.
WALT WHITMAN

Victor or victim

We can either exercise control over our lives or lose precious time as victims of circumstances.

A very close friend expressed to me recently the numbness she felt after her husband left her. The security and routines she had known for so many years suddenly fell to pieces and she was faced with nothing but the unknown and a very deflated ego. She was so angry and hurt that for months she was unable to make even the simplest decisions and was amazed by the advice of family and friends that she try new things, create new friendships, reawaken dormant talents and even find new love interests.

Trapped in her worthless preoccupation with sorting out what happened and who was to blame, she was going nowhere, except perhaps into depression. She refused to understand that it was her negative self-image over a lost love that prevented her from coming back to life. It took her months of wasted time and energy to realize that *moving on* was far more productive and exciting than *hanging on*.

There is no reason why we should always equate "ending" with "failure." Loss of love is always devastating, but it can also be a time for airing out stuffy inner rooms, reassessing values, starting anew. Relationships may become stagnant or wither and die, but life and love continue.

We don't make mistakes. We just have learnings.
ANNE WILSON SCHAEF

Having the
capacity to love is
not the same as
having the ability
to love.

Change for the sake of love

Unless we are willing to change, the possibility of sustaining a long lasting relationship is slim. When two comparative strangers make a commitment to unite, each brings a unique history, beliefs and habits. Some will be highly incompatible. If the relationship is to survive, it will mean that we will have to compromise, adjust, and be flexible.

One way to accomplish this is to listen to ourselves more often; listen to all our dead-ended statements: "Well, that's just the way I am," "I'm too old to change," "There is nothing I can do about it," "I can't," "I won't," "It's not my problem." Linguists tell us that the danger of using such language is that we become what we say we are and do only what we believe we can.

Love will never be the wonder that it can be if we continually confine ourselves. As long as we ignore alternatives or blame others for our problems, we will see ourselves as helpless or hopeless victims. Such actions drive away the very people we want to bring closer.

I know of no more encouraging fact than the unquestionable ability of man to elevate his life by conscious endeavor.
HENRY DAVID THOREAU

Love is also pain

It is often difficult to imagine that there is anything good about pain. The moment we feel it, we look for immediate relief. We take drugs, drown ourselves in alcohol, overeat, oversleep, suppress it, deny it—anything to keep from feeling discomfort.

To enter into a relationship is to court pain. This is all the more true when we approach others with preconceptions and expectations. Most want a lover to be our best friend, our closest confidant, our major source of happiness, an entertainer, someone who is forever understanding and forgiving. We want them to be loyal, exciting and sexy. Unfortunately, people answering those descriptions are usually found only in romance novels or in heaven. They are certainly rare on this earth. Accepting this, we know we are bound to experience the pain that comes from these unfulfilled expectations.

But pain is a great teacher. Just as physical pain can mobilize our defenses and alert us to deeper problems, so can emotional pain. It has the function of awakening us to the realization that there is something wrong in our lives, something that needs attention. If we ignore inner pain, it will surely grow out of control.

When we are as accepting of our pain, sorrow and disappointment as we are of our joys, we will be on our way to becoming real lovers.

Problems are messages.
SHAKTI GAWAIN

It takes maturity to love

I have come to the conclusion that the number of years we have lived has very little to do with maturity. There are children with more sensitivity and sense of responsibility than those who are raising them.

Maturity entails a great deal more than just reaching full growth. It means we have developed not only our mind, but emotional sensitivity as well. It requires courage to face life's challenges and intelligence to accept the unchangeable. It means attempting to understand human behavior even though it continues to baffle and frustrate us.

The mature person knows there are many ways, many solutions, many conclusions.

Love doesn't insist on perfection. But it does require us to realize the important correlation between who we are, what we believe, and how we behave.

Take your life in your hands and what happens?
A terrible thing: no one to blame.
ERICA JONG

If it seems that love has let you down

Anyone who has ever loved has felt its sting. When we enter into a relationship, we hope we will get what we want. When our desires meet in compatibility, there is love. When they conflict, there is confrontation. Even love cowers under such relentless pressures.

It is natural to want to avoid repeated painful experiences. We become overly cautious or shy away from anything that even hints at potential pain. We seclude ourselves behind defensive walls and in so doing feel that we can escape the perils of intimacy.

There may be comfort in retreat, but it doesn't last long. The reality is that we cannot live without people, nor can we live without love. So when relationships end, we have no choice but to start again. We must get up and get out. Lovers will not search for us in fairy tale castles, and knights in shining armor are long gone. The best way to come back to life is to give it. It will take time to pick up the pieces, but having experienced the puzzle will make it easier to develop a new pattern next time.

Remember that it wasn't love that put our lives on hold. Like life itself, love is always there, waiting, as challenging and promising as ever.

I think that these difficult times have helped me to understand better than before how infinitely rich and beautiful life is in every way and that so many things that one goes around worrying about are of no importance whatsoever.
ISAK DINESEN

*N*agging *ourselves out of love*

It's hard to love someone when they're nagging you. Nothing can be as persistently annoying and ineffectual. Still, with distressing regularity, we hear people who should know better nagging away at each other, convinced that somehow they are actually communicating.

"How many times must I tell you?" they whine.

"Will you ever finish that?" they say with a sigh.

"I hate to have to remind you again, but..."

"The trouble with you is . . . ," they state emphatically, as if they surely knew.

And on and on.

What there is to be gained from such statements beyond guilt, resentment, and animosity, escapes me. It seems almost sadistic to so berate someone in the name of love. Society will punish us enough if we make mistakes. We don't need additional anxiety poured on by those to whom we look for support.

The role of the lover is to be there to bandage the wound with care and concern; not to reopen it with useless, mind-warping, ear-piercing, nerve-shattering *nagging*.

Treat your wife like a thoroughbred and she'll never be a nag.
BUMPER STICKER

Love and anger

The person who tells us they never get angry is either a liar or a potential time bomb. It's best to avoid both. Anger, in varying degrees, is part of every relationship. It cannot be ignored or wished away.

Anger need not be destructive if it is expressed creatively and honestly. Most of us disguise it, try to sublimate it, suppress it or project it somewhere other than where it really belongs. These are common and sometimes successful outlets. It is healthier, however, to focus upon the cause of the anger rather than the anger itself. When anger is accepted as a natural human experience, it can be dealt with if expressed in a healthy manner. When we repress our anger, it eventually explodes with greater intensity, far out of proportion to the original provocation, leaving in its wake equally magnified resentment.

Mature individuals feel comfortable in dealing with their anger because they know it requires expression. Once expressed, it is often quickly and permanently relieved. If repressed, it always festers and finds expression in calamity.

Sometimes it's worse to win a fight than to lose.
BILLIE HOLIDAY

If we don't act upon
our madness in the
fanciful sense, we will
surely go mad in the
classical sense.

*L*ove can only be understood in action

It never occurred to my Mama to define love. She would have laughed at the idea. Everything she did was a kind of loving act. She gave love in our home a tangible feeling. Her love for her children and husband was plainly evident. She was forever looking at us fondly, hugging us (over our false protestations), or sharing in our laughter or tears. She never saw my Papa as a saint, but she treated him as a very likely candidate. You could feel her high level of spiritual love; her every act, thought and deed was an affirmation of the presence of God.

Love, for Mama, was not something she thought or talked about. It was something she lived in action. She showed us, as Mother Teresa has, that love is found in sweeping a floor, cleaning a sink, caring for someone ill, or offering a comforting embrace.

Mama, without trying, taught us the greatest, most enduring lesson of our lives: that love is far more than a feeling. It is something to be lived and acted upon, day in and day out.

All that is necessary to make this world a better place to live is to
love . . . to love as Christ loved, as Buddha loved.
ISADORA DUNCAN

Basic love words that count

It is the most twisted of logic to say, "Knowing you intimately means I can trample on your feelings."

We are often more considerate and understanding of total strangers than we are of our wives, husbands and children. Curiously, true consideration and genuine affection often seem reserved for insignificant, rather than significant others. When it comes to loved ones, people feel they never have to say that they are sorry and seldom say thank you. The words we use with them or the consequences of the remarks we make are rarely weighed. The people who do the most for us often become the least appreciated.

I once gave an assignment to my Love Class students to go home and simply say "thank you" to their parents. There were strong reservations about this project. They didn't feel it appropriate to thank their parents for anything. "Parents don't need our gratitude just for doing their duty. They know how we feel anyway," they protested. Nevertheless, I insisted that they complete the assignment, and share their findings with the class. I found the results predictable. The students, however, were astonished. Nearly every one of them found that their one simple expression of gratitude made a real impact. After recovering from the initial shock, the parents were overjoyed! Some actually cried with unexpected delight and surprise.

A kind word, sincerely stated, can work magic, most notably in relationships where the magic is gone. We are never so sophisticated or so comfortable in a relationship that the little niceties can be neglected. If they are good enough for total strangers, they are certainly good enough for the people we love.

The only way to speak the truth is to speak lovingly.
HENRY DAVID THOREAU

Don't worry about tomorrow

No one has the power to foretell the future. I think it's best that this is true. Take away the elements of surprise and mystery and our lives would be long and boring. The inability to predict even the next moment is only a problem when we insist on imagining the worst.

Many of us get our emotional exercise jumping to negative conclusions. We conjure grim faces through every window and around every corner. In so doing, we withdraw from possible opportunities for enhancement and joy, and project problems where they do not exist. We reject positive advances from a friend or loved one because we are convinced they have ulterior motives. In turn, we imagine that if *we* reach out to someone, we will similarly be rejected. So we never take the chance that may result in our greatest advancement.

The future is where we will spend the rest of our lives and it is our choice whether we look forward with confidence and courage or walk blindfolded toward some nebulous impending doom. Since tomorrows have a way of suddenly and dramatically becoming todays, it is to our advantage to live more in the present and let tomorrow tell its own tale.

Don't be afraid your life will end,
be afraid that it will never begin.
GRACE HANSEN

If you don't love everybody, you don't really love anybody

I was on a popular late night television show once where it was obvious from the moment I walked onto the set that the host had little or no knowledge of who I was or what I believed. He was convinced that anyone who taught a love class must be somewhat demented and he was determined to approach the interview as a big joke.

"Is it true that you say we should love everyone?" he asked incredulously.

"Yes. I'd say that was a fair statement," I responded.

"Well," he laughed. "That's not only crazy, it's impossible. I don't love everyone. I don't even want to."

"That's your privilege," I told him. "But whom would you exclude? And for what reason?"

As verbal as he was, he was speechless.

I am convinced that when we truly understand the truth of loving and accept universal vulnerability of humankind, we can develop empathy for even the unlovable.

Love means the ability to identify with imperfection and to recognize the inadequacies, weaknesses, fears and confusion in ourselves and others. Loving what is unlovable in them is always a challenge. It's so much easier to dismiss people for their failings than it is to stick by them. I wonder why it is that we are more prone to finding fatal flaws than looking for redeeming qualities?

We do not love people so much for the good
they have done us, as for the good we have done them.
LEO TOLSTOY

Love as a confidence builder

It is interesting that those who seem to make it most difficult for us to love them are often the most in need of love. A friend recently laughed that her teen-age son tests the limits of her love almost daily. I offered my opinion that he would be giving up his unwashed, neon muscle shirt and tri-colored Mohawk hairdo in good time, but she didn't really need my assurances. She had already learned the importance of standing by him and allowing him to move through the necessary stages of growth. She knew from experience what was truly important: a flexible outlook, an understanding heart, plenty of love, and the quiet confidence that everything would turn out just fine.

Of course, it's not just the young among us who need this kind of understanding. We can all benefit from the knowledge that people believe in us, respect us and are able to see our changing behaviors as positive signs of growth.

Remember always that you have not only the right to be an individual, you have an obligation to be one.
ELEANOR ROOSEVELT

All the things
that "go without saying" or
that are "understood"
between two people in love
can build up a mountain
of miscommunication.

Coercion and loving

There are still people who believe that love can be received or restrained by means of coercion. They would run us through a maze of "musts" and "shoulds" until we are made to feel obliged to love on their terms or lose them. These "lovers" burden us with guilt and fear until we cower under their pressures. Too often they succeed. They clip our wings, relegate us to a comfortable cage where they can parcel out their love to us according to their whims and needs.

Thoreau suggested that birds never sing in caves. Neither do human beings. We were born free and are entitled to love without coercion and without constraint. Any other arrangement is an imitation, if not a distortion of love.

No one has ever forced love from another and never will. Love liberates and releases us to live fully without fear and without the constant need to conform to the designs of another.

Coercion depletes. Love empowers us to move consciously and resolutely toward ever greater freedom.

To enjoy freedom we have to control ourselves.
VIRGINIA WOOLF

*L*ove needs encouragement

Healthy, earnest and positive encouragement is far more effective than the usual criticism we so freely offer our loved ones. Disparaging remarks, accusations, and complaints do get attention, but often at a price.

I recently heard a mother in a supermarket reprimanding her child. "Watch what you're doing, stupid!" she said. "You're so clumsy! You'll never amount to anything." One wonders about the cumulative effect of repeatedly hearing this kind of message.

We all have a certain level of nobility and respond positively to being treated with respect. A word of encouragement at the right moment can work magic. Phrases such as, "You can do it!" "Good for you!" "Well done!" "I'm proud of you," have power to nurture and help us to bloom. We can all become more. Gentle encouragement builds confidence and promotes growth. Negative criticism tears down and, over time, reinforces the same negative acts it attempts to correct.

Too many people miss the silver
lining because they're expecting gold.
MAURICE SETTER

Celebrating our differences

Each of us brings to our life a unique temperament and style. This is our special gift to the world. How monotonous it would be if we all expressed ourselves in similar predictable ways. Difference is the spice of human behavior that makes us so fascinating.

Some of us charge boldly through life taking risks; others choose to play it safe. Some of us are eager for social interactions; others are more contented being loners. Some are spontaneous; others are planned. Some approach each day with gusto; others are cautious. Some are perfectionists; others are less exacting. In love we become acutely aware of these differences and are careful not to force our values upon those with different behaviors.

Our love makes room for everyone. As long as we remain open to differences, we are constantly enriched. There are as many approaches to life as there are people in this world. The more of these ways we can understand and accept, the more full and loving our love becomes.

The French say, "Vive la difference." Love echoes the phrase.

It is possible to be different and still be all right.
ANNE WILSON SCHAEF

Love and new beginnings

The essence of life is renewal. If we are truly alive, we are reborn every day. We cannot assimilate even the most insignificant thing without being affected by the experience. Every minute offers the potential for newness and discovery; for realization and actualization; for new opportunities to love and be loved.

We spend most of our lives among the same people day in and day out. On the surface, they appear unchanging and it does not occur to us that perhaps beneath their surface a whole world of change may be going on, undetected and unappreciated.

Even if we resist change, it is said that at the moment we are born we are already moving on our inevitable path to death. It is no secret that our bodies undergo dramatic changes; it should be as acceptable that our minds, our tastes, our opinions, our beliefs and our dreams are also changing each day.

Lovers know that they can never assume anything about the people they love. They must allow each person, each object, each day, each moment, to tell its own story. They know that their senses may betray them, but that through love they are encouraged toward the acceptance of a lifetime of new beginnings.

People change and don't tell each other.
LILLIAN HELLMAN

Love and patience

Nothing nurtures love more than patience. It is that quality that allows us to wait, to understand, to hope. It sometimes seems this is all but forgotten in a world that is forever on fast forward.

Patience denotes self-composure and contemplation in the face of disappointments and failures. Nevertheless, we want action, we want solutions, we want answers. And we want them at once. This philosophy has been responsible for many hasty judgments which have caused a great deal of unnecessary pain and despair.

In love, the most vital answers take time for discovery, time that is sustained by hope and absence of pressures. Many of our problems are only stalking shadows that often disappear in the light of patience. People who love well and love long have learned to accept the times of discomfort along with the moments of sublime joy.

The greatest reward of patience is a love that endures.

The way to love anything is to realize it might be lost.
G.K. CHESTERTON

*F*ocusing on possibility

Lovers always focus away from negativity, to beauty, goodness and joy. Though they are aware of the dark side of life, they avoid gravitating to it. Obsession with what is wrong with the world assures our blindness to what is good and right. On the other hand, solutions become more visible in the light of possibilities.

Beauty and goodness are successful forces against ugliness and evil. Negative people look for (and always find) confirmation for the negative, just as positive people look for and find the lightness of being. Both exist. Both are real and are always with us. The difference is as basic as a decision, and as simple as opening our eyes.

Prosocial behavior of all sorts, including altruism, is so
normal and expected that we scarcely notice, but are
struck by its absence or opposite. Cruelty is
attention getting, kindness unremarkable.
MORTON HUNT

The fun of loving

Our first love is often the high point of our lives. We are too preoccupied to eat, we sleep fitfully, and our thoughts are too filled with love to act rationally about anything *except* our love. We feel wonderfully miserable, totally out of control. Everything seems perfect, beautiful beyond description. Days are magical, full of tenderness, laughter and surprise. And then, after a period of time, we often outgrow the very things that made love so special. We ask ourselves, "What happened to the joy of loving? How could I ever have seen it as fun? Where and why did the joy vanish?" Fun has nearly evaporated, having bowed out in deference to the rules of sound adult behavior. Impetuousness and spontaneity have become casualties of logic and responsibility.

Love is not all that serious. The fun of loving can be brought back again when we are willing to transcend the predictable and again embrace the paradoxical and illogical reasoning that is such an essential part of love.

We remain true to the ideal of love by never allowing ourselves to forget the laughter, humor and surprise that was so much a part of love's first experience.

In trying to win, we feel a loss. Feeling the loss,
we see that we are one. Seeing we are one, we desire to play.
In beginning to play, we open to love.
O. FRED DONALDSON

Excellence is
the pursuit of
perfection, not its
achievement.

Needing is different from loving

We all love to be needed, but few enjoy being desperately needed. Part of loving lies in the joy of being with people with whom we share deeply, who care about us and will support us even when we may be wrong, confused or despondent. Need becomes neurotic, however, when others use us to fulfill themselves. None of us need the responsibility of those who give themselves totally to us. The load is too heavy.

Fortunately, love is self-fulfilling. We become complete only through our own efforts. Neurotic need implies a lack that can only be filled by someone else. Loving means standing on our own two feet, counting on ourselves, making our own way. We may, at times, need the help of others, but we cannot expect them to satisfy needs which are solely ours to satisfy.

To be emotionally committed to somebody is very difficult,
but to be alone is impossible.
STEPHEN SONDHEIM

228

Love is in the attitude

The important thing is not what happens to us, but how we respond to it. We have very little control over what other people say or do, what catastrophes nature may bring or that we all will age and die. But we have all the control in the world over how we respond to these things.

We should all acknowledge that we are fully responsible for our beliefs, attitudes and behaviors. Being loveless, for example, is not a mean trick that life has played upon us. More likely, it is a conscious decision on our part to close love out. It's often easier to think of ourselves as victims of a cruel fate than to accept our part in the problem. But it's neither accurate nor conducive to bringing love back into our lives to ignore that we were at least partly responsible.

There is a Zen koan which states:

My barn having burned down,
I can now see the moon.

Is the barn's destruction a catastrophe or an advantage? Right you are if you think you are.

There is nothing good or bad, but thinking makes it so.
WILLIAM SHAKESPEARE

*L*ove is immortal

Death is the ultimate equalizer, reducing us all to a common fate. What will distinguish us are the memories we leave behind.

I was deeply moved by a statement made by one of my nephews after the death of my father. He said simply, but with determination, "Grandpa isn't dead. I won't let him die!"

This may have come from the mouth of a babe, but it is nonetheless true. As long as there is someone who loves us, we will remain alive. Memories make us immortal. In truth, love will outlive even memories.

To live in hearts we leave behind is not to die.
THOMAS CAMPBELL

Awareness of our changing roles

When I was growing up, sex roles, to the detriment of both, were clearly delineated. The male was the aggressor, the provider, the protector, the unfeeling. The female was to be the more yielding and helpless, while being the nurturer. Any deviation from these clearly defined roles placed one on dangerous ground.

Few questioned these roles, though some were uncomfortable with them. So clearly were the roles defined and so completely were they accepted, that even psychological tests were constructed upon these prejudices. Men were not expected to enjoy opera or ballet or a good book and women were not to express interest in weight lifting, basketball or corporate competitions.

It's not surprising that such outrageous and outmoded concepts have not withstood the scrutiny of a more enlightened society. The more they are analyzed, the more incredulous they seem. Why shouldn't men cry, cook, enjoy opera? Why shouldn't women be the major providers, lift weights and love baseball?

Love disregards roles. It encourages both men and women to discover their natural needs, find their real selves, and express their uniqueness as human beings. From this, everyone benefits, not only from having greater freedom, but also in the pride of a more enlightened love.

The greatest discovery of my generation is that human beings can alter their lives by altering their attitudes of mind.
WILLIAM JAMES

Making love felt

The majority of us lead quiet, unheralded lives as we pass through this world. There will most likely be no ticker-tape parades for us, no monuments created in our honor. But that does not lessen our possible impact upon the world, for there are scores of people waiting for someone just like us to come along; people who will appreciate our compassion, our encouragement, who will need our unique talents. Someone who will live a happier life merely because we took the time to share what we had to give.

Too often we underestimate the power of a touch, a smile, a kind word, a listening ear, an honest compliment, or the smallest act of caring, all of which have the potential to turn a life around. It's overwhelming to consider the continuous opportunities there are to make our love felt.

Service isn't a big thing. It's a million little things.
ANONYMOUS

Those who think
they know it all have
no way of finding
out they don't.

You are what you do

If everyone who purported to be a lover were to put it in action, this would be a much improved world. It is an old truth that if we really want to know someone, we should be less concerned with what they say, and more alert to what they do. That is why love is a verb. What is going on inside of us is revealed by what we are doing outside.

If we truly love, how are we demonstrating this? If we care deeply for our family, our children, how are we making this evident? If we are honestly concerned with hunger, poverty, loneliness, violence in the world, how are we showing this concern? If there is no tangible evidence of our love in action, then it is doubtful that we are loving.

I once sat next to a man on an airplane who complained across the entire continent. The flight attendants were useless, the food was terrible, the seating was cramped, the movie was lousy. Then he sank his teeth into larger issues: the government was corrupt, society was rotten, people were not to be trusted, on and on! During our conversation, I mentioned that my focus was the study and enhancement of love. He snapped to attention. "That's great! What the world needs is more love," he assured me. Then, without pausing, he added, "It's a good thing that there are still people like you and me who understand that."

You will know them by their fruits.
MATTHEW 7:16

*O*n making mistakes

Some of us are paralyzed at the possibility of making a mistake. We act as if our errors are like watercolors which, once brushed on, sink indelibly into the paper, set forever with no possibility of being rectified. Being so inclined, we make even insignificant decisions traumatic experiences. Eventually, such people ruled by their inactivity and indecision, must put their lives on hold.

On the other hand, there are those who see their errors as opportunities. When they make mistakes, they are not suspended in agony, nor do they stop trusting themselves.

It may be comforting to note that everyone, no matter how wise or sensitive, makes mistakes, and what is more, will probably continue to do so. So why not relax, accept your imperfections and join the human race?

A life spent in making mistakes is not only more honorable, but more useful than a life spent in doing nothing.
GEORGE BERNARD SHAW

Self-respect

When we have a healthy respect for ourselves, there is no limit to what we can succeed in doing. When we believe that everything is possible for us, accomplishment becomes natural.

No one knows better than we what is essential for our own growth and happiness. Those who direct their own lives don't depend upon kindly gnomes or favorable alignment of the planets. They use knowledge, experience, hard work, belief in themselves, and optimism to achieve their goals.

There are no barriers to our dreams so long as we believe in ourselves as the source of our happiness. We will be on the way to having what we want when we have set our minds to believing we can get it, and not a moment sooner.

Whether you think you can or you
think you can't, you are right.
HENRY FORD

Surviving conflicts

We are often more adroit at handling world-shaking conflicts than we are at handling simple interpersonal ones. When our lives appear to fill with contradictions and frustrations, we are often pitifully unprepared to work out solutions. We want to be guided by reason, but we are often overruled by our passions, resulting in an ongoing battle with ourselves—one that never results in a decisive victory.

We are nothing more than slaves to our feelings until we learn to better understand and control them. Feelings without reason only give rise to confusion and disorder.

It is not necessary to constantly apologize for what we feel. Love is born of feelings, but it is nurtured through intellect. When balanced, these two essential ingredients will assure our growth in love as well as its survival.

The head never rules the heart,
but just becomes its partner in crime.
MIGNON MCLAUGHLIN

Love and cooperation

We need each other. We cannot succeed alone. What is the good of being successful if there is no one to acknowledge it or celebrate it with us?

We require the support of those we love, and they need us. We live better, healthier and longer lives by working together than we do by working apart. Total self-sufficiency is an egotistical illusion. There is far more strength in cooperation. By seeking what another needs, we can determine how we can best help them. In the process, we are sure to discover that it is impossible to enhance the life of another without benefiting ourselves.

Coming together is a beginning. Keeping together is a progress.
Working together is success.
ANONYMOUS

Love is the prize of the strong

It takes great courage to love. Though it is often perceived to be effortless, anyone who has ever loved would maintain that it is anything but that. By its nature, love requires that we risk rejection, overcome barriers of resistance, surmount our weaknesses and fully utilize our resources. If we are rejected, we will need courage to rise up and try again. If we are hurt, we must have the confidence that we will heal. If we are desolate, we must muster up the human dignity to prevail.

With the courage to meet whatever hindrances we may encounter along the way, we become more than just "re-actors" to our lives; we become the actors who determine their courses.

You don't get to choose how you're going to die, or when.
You can only decide how you're going to live. Now.
JOAN BAEZ

Success in love

There is no instant success in love. Like any other success in life, it can only be determined after the fact. For certain, success comes gradually, one step at a time, each move forward serving to enhance the next, each advancement or failure serving to prepare for things to come.

Though relationships may be made in heaven, they surely have to be worked out on earth. They demand determined effort and total commitment to survive moments of indifference and neglect. They will grow when two people move together in love and will not cease to grow, even in times when the direction seems unclear.

Only in looking back can we tell love's real story, but we are creating that story each year, each month, each day, each hour, now!

If you want the present and the future to be different from the past, Spinosa tells us, study the past, find out the causes that made it what it was and bring different causes to bear.
WILL AND ARIEL DURANT

*L*ove and tears

It is always refreshing when science gets around to confirming something we have felt instinctively. For instance, I recently read of a study about adult crying. The scientific research indicated that tears of emotion contain one of the brain chemicals known to be pain killers and, therefore, should be encouraged in time of pain.

As we all know, when we are in the midst of trials, there is little comfort in being told that, "this too shall pass," or that we should maintain a stiff upper lip, or that love will eventually intervene and heal us. In the meantime, there is nothing quite so satisfying, and so healing, as a good cry.

Those who do not know how to weep with their whole heart,
don't know how to laugh either.
GOLDA MEIR

The notion that there might be a better or more convenient time to love has cost many people a lifetime of regret.

The face of love

If you are always concerned that you won't have the right words, you can still take heart. Psychologist Albert Fehrabian tells us that communication is seven percent verbal, thirty-eight percent vocal and fifty-five percent facial. The words we use, he suggests, say less than our facial expressions.

I vividly recall learning to read my parents' faces when I was growing up, for survival's sake. Papa had a certain smile that would ripen into a glow of satisfaction that was impossible to misinterpret. A wrinkled brow and lowered eyelids told us, unmistakenly, to beware. Mama had a way of rolling her eyes upward and shaking her head from side to side that told us it was definitely time to be quiet. They, of course, also had a wonderful way of showing their love, which I can still see when I recall their faces.

It is a good idea to give some thought to how our faces are reflecting what we are saying and thinking. I always ask friends how they are when I greet them. They often answer, "Fine!" with a scowl. "Well, then why don't you tell your face?" I wonder.

*The world is a looking glass and gives back to every
man the reflection of his own face.
WILLIAM THACKERAY*

A gift of love

Love is always bestowed as a gift—freely, willingly, and without expectation. It is offered even when not acknowledged or appreciated. We don't love to be loved, we love to love.

He who wants to do good, knocks at the gate.
He who loves, finds the gate open.
RABINDRANATH TAGORE

On educating for love

I recently heard a professional educator expounding on the ills of education. He was directing his remarks to young adults and their challenge to meet the demands of tomorrow. What he said made sense, but it left an incomplete picture and left me feeling frustrated and sad. He said that knowledge was doubling every three years and that educators were unable to cope with the challenge. Regretfully, he omitted saying that tomorrow's adults more than ever will need to learn how to be loving human beings. He said nothing about the need to cultivate sensitivity, responsibility, commitment to other people and to our environment.

It seemed to me that if our knowledge becomes dated so quickly, much of it must be transitory. Perhaps we should be telling our children that not all knowledge becomes obsolete overnight; that there are truths that transcend our books and changing beliefs. Surely teaching about the latest technology and how to be successful do not preclude also teaching a sense of goodness, gentleness, giving, caring, spirituality and love. These alone remain our fixed truths, essential for human survival, as well as technical success, even in today's fast-changing world.

Let us not be a generation recorded in future
histories as destroying the irreplaceable inheritance
of life formed through eons past.
CHARLES A. LINDBERGH

Love's insurance

I heard a story about a wife who was determined to get back at her neglectful mate. She felt ignored, wronged and betrayed. Since it wasn't in her nature to act out or verbalize her frustration in spiteful, vicious ways, she decided to shower her husband with affection and compliments, kill him with kindness and love.

Her plan had surprising effects. It soon became apparent that the marriage took on a different aura. As a result of her new and unexpected expressions of caring, her husband began to reciprocate in kind. They suddenly discovered something which had been missing in their relationship— the continual assurance of love.

Love is always made more manifest through continual demonstrations.

Kindness in words creates confidence. Kindness in thinking creates profoundness. Kindness in giving creates love.
LAO-TZU

Gentleness and love

Thomas Aquinas, who knew a great deal about gentleness, once said that when you want to convert someone to your view, go over to them, take them by the hand and guide them. You don't stand at a distance and shout at them; you don't call them names or demand that they come to where you are. You must start from where they are. That's the best way, he assures us, to get them to rethink their viewpoint and perhaps change their position.

While it is true that most people respect strength, they don't always associate it with gentleness. But it is always from strength that gentleness arises. It is always from strength that we learn not to condemn weakness or fear or anger. Strength encourages us to empathize, to be more adaptable and make allowances. If we really wish to bring someone into our hearts and minds, a little gentleness is a powerful attraction.

Do not use a hatchet to
remove a fly from your friend's forehead.
A CHINESE PROVERB

Yielding

Prior to entering into a relationship it is well to ask ourselves how much we are willing to compromise. If we feel completely integrated as individuals, unwilling to adjust, perhaps we'd avoid a great deal of unhappiness by going it alone.

I have never understood the value of proving our brilliance if we wound the one we love. Why is it so important that we are unwavering in our beliefs if they continually threaten the relationships we value? Is it so necessary to always be right if it continually causes resentment and ill will?

Of course, there should be some limitations to our flexibility and willingness to compromise. But we are rarely asked to give up what is truly essential about ourselves. A little consideration is mainly what most people need from us. This amounts to knowing when to act or not act, when to speak our mind or be silent, when to give in and when to stand firm, when to set our limits or extend them. We're wise in love when we have achieved a balance between our willingness to yield and the knowledge of how far to go before we are harming ourselves and others in the process.

Winning is overemphasized. The only time it is
really important is in surgery and war.
AL MCGUIRE

The environment of love

If we are wise, we strive to create our loving environment. We are content where passion does not overshadow fondness; where physical needs are no more important than emotional needs. Differences are celebrated here, not just tolerated, and respect grows instead of being allowed to erode. This is a place where there is real sharing rather than indifference. This loving environment encourages when nothing else does and nourishes like nothing else can.

Man shapes himself through
decisions that shape his environment.
RENÉ DUBOIS

Love and freedom

Freedom entails choice, responsibility and commitment, and, as such, doesn't come free. It always demands a price. We cannot love without relinquishing something in the process. Some people may see this as a form of enslavement, an abandoning of freedom. But when we love, we do so with personal commitment, volitionally. When we give of ourselves, we are freed from the prison of self-absorption, so the more we give, the freer we become.

Freedom is nothing else but a chance to be better.
ALBERT CAMUS

It is when we ask for
love less and begin
giving it more that the
secret of human love
is revealed to us.

F ear of loving

One of the greatest deterrents to love is fear. At times it makes cowards of us all. It causes us to take the safe path, to slink from commitment, to hide from ourselves and others. There, in our haven of safety, we isolate ourselves from the very things that give life joy and meaning.

Confronting our fears does not mean retreating from involvement any more than it means developing a tough exterior to be impervious to pain. Allowing fear to determine the course of our lives is to listen to only one of our inner voices. Other voices also deserve to be heard. One of them is saying that the worst fear we face is a life deprived of love. Where love exists strongly enough, apprehension, disappointment, and fear are reduced to nothing.

Nothing in life is to be feared. It is only to be understood.
MARIE CURIE

*D*on't make today's judgments based upon yesterday's memories

There is little doubt that we are largely products of our memories. Without our being fully aware of it, past experiences have a way of weaving themselves into an ever expanding web of entrapment, ensnaring our present view of life. Before we are, we were, so new ideas are filtered through past beliefs. When we attempt to establish what is, we are bogged down by what was.

But there is hope. No one is permanently preprogrammed. We all have the ability to assimilate new experience. But to do so, we must battle our memories and lessen their power. Unless we want our future to be nothing more than a rehash of our past, we must be aware of the power of the past to affect our behavior. Only then can we be free to create our future.

Our memory is a monster; You forget . . . it doesn't.
It simply files things away. It keeps things for you or hides things
from you . . . and summons to your recall with a will of its own.
You think you have a memory, but it has you!
JOHN IRVING

The pleasure of love

We endure a great deal for love because we know that the end result is extremely pleasurable. In fact, there is perhaps no emotion we can imagine that is more totally satisfying.

It is when we are in love that we experience our most profound feelings of joy and peace, our greatest security and our deepest knowledge of the wonder of oneness. Love is reinforced by the promise of these pleasures and we continue to love in their anticipation.

If there is a problem, it arises from the fact that we are taught to be suspicious of pleasure. We are told that it is an illusion, even that it is sinful. We are made to feel guilty when we experience it, in spite of the fact that pleasure is the great motivator for our continuing search for love. Pleasure is love's sweet reward.

*Man, unlike the animals, has never learned that
the sole purpose of life is to enjoy it.*
SAMUEL BUTLER

Love and opportunity

If we are love starved, it is because we have narrow definitions of it. Happily, opportunity does knock more than once when it comes to love. Otherwise, we'd all be very sorry, loveless individuals.

Love is persistent. It keeps knocking, offering to embrace and be embraced and share its wonder. All it requires of us is that we remain receptive. There are opportunities for love in every act we perform.

We often miss the opportunity to love because love assumes many disguises, often unrecognizable to us at the moment. Our myths and fairy tales are full of such examples. They ask, would you kiss a frog? Tend to some noisy, old dwarfs? Risk the yellow brick road? Duel with dragons? Travel the world over?

Of course, there are less exotic opportunities that present themselves to us every day of our lives. We are free to take them or decline them as we choose. But those who cry about looking for love in all the wrong places might be better off to stop crying and try opening their eyes a little wider.

Hold fast to dreams, for if dreams die,
life is a broken winged bird that cannot fly.
LANGSTON HUGHES

*A*ppreciation for love

A very creative and resourceful teacher friend found that great changes took place among her students when she took time each day to point out something positive about them. In addition, once a week she had a "sharing good things" time. This consisted of each child paying someone a compliment. This became a favorite activity for the positive atmosphere it created, an environment that was reflected in the greater personal dignity of each student.

It actually takes very little to make people happy or raise their self-esteem. All that's required is an educated heart and kindness mixed with honesty and style.

The deepest principle of human natures
is the craving to be appreciated.
WILLIAM JAMES

Planning for love

It is a wonderful, romantic notion that love thrives upon serendipity and spontaneity. To some degree, this is indeed true and one would hope that they would always be a part of a loving relationship. But there is no harm in bringing some sort of order into our lives as well. It never hurts to consider early in a relationship how we plan to enhance it, or those things we are determined to avoid that could diminish it.

Actually, part of the fun of love lies in dreaming of the future together. This does not imply elaborate blueprints or rigid goals. Rather, it suggests allowing tomorrow to enter our consciousness by considering it today.

In the story of *Candide*, Voltaire has his hero and heroine plan their loving future together. They are each too ego-centered to listen to the other. Her dream is for pearls, ruby rings and palaces with marble swimming pools. His goal is to live simply on a few acres of land with a pig, a cow and a vegetable garden. They both expect, quite unrealistically, that love will bridge the differences.

Preparing for a lifetime together means more than two lovers lost in each other's arms leaving their glorious future to heaven. Planning does not preclude joy and wonder, it clears the way for it.

*Planning is bringing the future into the present
so that you can do something about it.*
ALAN LAKEIN

Security and love

Everyone would like a guarantee that their love will last. We even take vows to that effect when we marry and declare our undying love publicly. It used to be that everyone was expected to fall in love forever. But the only thing we can be certain of is that there will be change. Whether dramatic or subtle, we can—and should—count on change.

Since we know that love offers no assurance, the only security we can know is that it is dynamic and will grow or die, depending upon how it is nurtured. Security lies in the acceptance of its changing nature. Knowing this, we have nothing to fear.

Only in growth, reform and change,
paradoxically enough, is true security to be had.
ANNE MORROW LINDBERGH

Love is not a
competitive sport.

Love profits from a sense of humor

It had been one of those long, draining days, to the point that getting together with friends seemed more like an obligation than a renewal. When I arrived for dinner, I was asked by my hosts if I would go upstairs and read to their four-year-old daughter. She had been excited all day about my coming. I was her favorite "uncle." I wasn't terribly thrilled about the prospect, but I'd never do anything to disappoint a child.

The book that little Carolyn handed me was her favorite which had already been read to her a hundred times. But with children, magic never gets old. It was the story of a giant pumpkin that turned into an automobile and of his journey with his best friends, the lizard and the owl. They roamed a countryside of pink grass and Jell-O trees, bumping into and picking up a host of outrageous characters along the way. As the two of us read and giggled over this wonderful nonsense, I couldn't help but feel the accumulated ill temper of the day fall away.

I was reminded that the little child, which we like to think always dwells within us, sometimes needs some coaxing to come out and play, if even for a brief moment, to take a mirthful trip with a pumpkin, an owl and a lizard.

Trying to make sense of this crazy, wonderful world certainly demands mountains of thoughtful consideration, steadiness and sober reflection, but just a touch of fun and fancy from time to time doesn't hurt either. The world profits from our madness every bit as much as it does our sanity.

Sanity is madness put to good use.
GEORGE SANTAYANA

Love and understanding

Love would be simplified if everything we believed were true and reality conformed to our perceptions. But perception is not like that. We see what we are prepared to see and believe what we want to believe. In a large sense, we are slaves to who we already are.

Understanding in love implies letting loose of expectations and perceptions by allowing what evidence of truth there is to present itself. It means being free of stereotypes and rigid prejudices and staying open to new experiences.

When we say we don't love something or someone, it usually means that we are unable to see it or them clearly. Coming to a better understanding is a slow, painstaking process, but the rewards are great. We may discover that though it can be painful to learn new things and change our antiquated beliefs, it is far more painful and costly in the long run, to remain static and unsympathetic.

Tolerance is the positive and cordial effort to understand
another's beliefs, practices, and habits without
necessarily sharing or accepting them.
JOSHUA LIEBMAN

Time to love

Time is a strange phenomenon. It is the great leveler, so democratic, so final. It is the most valuable commodity we have. No one can steal it from us without our permission. It moves on steadily and we are helpless to stop it. We are often careless about each moment, since tomorrow's supply of time is assumed to be waiting.

The question is: how much time are we willing to devote to love? The answer will depend, of course, upon the value we put on loving.

It is well to remember that love, like time, does not wait for anyone.

We always have enough time, if we but use it aright.
JOHANN WOLFGANG VON GOETHE

Love is in need of solitude

There is a beautiful and wise saying that "God mainly speaks in whispers." Our environment is so often filled with distracting static that we are not often privy to God's whispers.

We need time alone to contemplate and meditate upon our lives, our feelings, our most secret thoughts and dreams. No matter how much we love or how much we enjoy the companionship of those we love, solitude is essential if we hope to have our love continue.

Papa and Mama had a wonderful escape from the endless chatter of their children. Each evening while we performed household chores, such as washing the dishes, cleaning the kitchen floor, and putting away leftovers, they would wander out into the night for an hour's walk. Though we all cried to accompany them, this was clearly designated as their private time. When we asked them what they did on these walks, they assured us that they didn't do anything. They just walked, looked at the stars, enjoyed the stillness and the pleasure of each other's company. We thought that was crazy! Why would anyone want to spend an hour counting stars?

That was many years ago. With a child's sensibilities, it was difficult to imagine ever needing private, quiet time. I can't tell you how many stars I've counted since then. My hunger for times of quiet aloneness never diminishes.

You will find that deep place of silence right in your
room, your garden or even your bathtub.
ELIZABETH KÚBLER ROSS

*L*ive love in the present

It is as useless to drag old concerns into the present as it is to fear the future. The only thing that really matters is how we are living our love at each moment. Even knowing this, we often waste so much energy on what was, and what will be that we have little time left for what is.

A young student of mine learned this lesson well. She told me that she was constantly worried about the future of her relationships to the point that she was always full of anxiety and in constant need of reassurance. She realized that her behavior was not healthy. This continual uncertainty actually pushed people away. Who wants to be with a person who is constantly fretting? She decided to relax. She stopped analyzing everything and began to enjoy what was happening to her at the time. Once people accepted the change, everything easily fell into place.

Those who believe in themselves, and trust in the moment, are those who find life most enjoyable. They have learned that the past is a place to store memories, not regrets; that the future should be full of promise, not apprehension. And the present is all we need.

The past must no longer be used as an
anvil for beating out the present and the future.
PAUL-EMILE BORDUAS

Compassion is an act of tolerance where kindness and forgiveness reign. When we make the compassionate choice, we enhance the dignity of each individual, which is the very essence of loving them.

The cumulative effect of our simple acts

Every act has its consequence. We may not be aware of its importance, but in some way, each event contributes to a bigger picture, the significance of which will be revealed only in time. If we can accept this, we can appreciate the importance of the simple, seemingly inconsequential acts we perform without thought, words we speak without consideration or hopes we dash without regard.

Only the past is immortal.
DELMORE SCHWARTZ

On being ourselves

It seems that everyone knows what's best for us. Listen and we will find that a lot of the communication we hear is advice. We are lectured, scolded, warned, preached at. We are told what we should be doing with our lives, how we should be thinking and what our goals should be. Daily, we encounter individuals who will cite impressive statistical data, trends, styles, and testimonials, all to confirm their ideas and entice us to their way of thinking.

There is always value in new information as long as we (a) really know its source, and (b) don't automatically rely on someone else's answers as being right for us.

We are all unique, with special needs and styles of living, loving and learning. Our lives are our own and we must be wary of anyone who attempts to seduce them from us.

There is no single way to love. There are as many expressions of caring, appreciation, and enhancement as there are people who have ever loved.

Our happiness is in us. At times we will need input, or special guidance, but this should only be as long as it takes to regain our balance and encourage us on our way.

Abasement, degradation is simply the manner of life of the man who has refused to be what it is his duty to be.
JOSÈ ORTEGA Y GASSET

When love loses its zest

Over time we have a way of taking each other for granted, falling into predictable routines and making what were once provocative actions into conventional ones. It's not really our fault, it's just that love seems most susceptible to this.

After years of two people being close, it's not uncommon to find that novelty is replaced with predictability. Spontaneity gives way to habit and routine. Where once being with that special person was always intriguing and adventurous, now it seems mechanical and monotonous. Fortunately love is easily rekindled with a little freshness and surprise.

I have a friend who is seen by many as being rather eccentric, but has found many special ways to keep her husband alert and interested. She is forever dreaming up crazy things that add spice to their lives, from suddenly greeting him at the door with an enticing negligee, to presenting him with inexpensive nonrefundable tickets on a cruise to exotica. His initial response is always one of annoyance, but he is soon won over by the sheer joy of it all. Their relationship continues to flourish. For them, the magic is never gone, they're still creating it.

Is not this the true romantic feeling . . . not to desire to escape
life, but to prevent life from escaping you?
THOMAS CLAYTON WOLFE

Love is fun

What has ever brought us greater joy than being in love? It makes us ever more alive to each moment, to the mystery, the unpredictability, to the grandiose yet playful feeling that the world is our toy.

Actually, love deepens our sense of humor. It makes us capable of laughing at the world and human behavior, especially our own. Loving behavior (though it may not have seemed so at the time), is often enormously funny. When we squint back at the adversity, it often brings a knowing smile. Our great seriousness over the trivia that often interferes with love is usually a laugh riot when we finally return to our senses.

If we are going to love, we will surely find plenty to laugh at.

I realize that humor isn't for everyone. It's only for people who
want to have fun, enjoy life, and feel alive.
ANNE WILSON SCHAEF

*E*ach day offers a new opportunity for love

We are told that there is nothing new under the sun. I have found this to be a great lie. In fact, each day everything is new under the sun! All things are either in the process of growing or dying, but nothing is remaining the same. Each morning when we awaken we can expect the day to be another boring interruption of our sleep, or we can take it as another opportunity to circulate a few new refreshing ideas. Each day has novelty written all over it if only we will awaken to it.

We are offered opportunities to create anew, to see in a different way, to change a little from the day before. If at the end of a day we are no different from when we started, we should beware. Sameness will surely create boredom and when we are bored, we are certain to be boring. What a waste in our dynamic universe!

Love grows by giving. The love we give away is the only love
we keep. The only way to retain love is to give it away.
ELBERT HUBBARD

The delicate balance of feeling

We are all emotional beings. We have feelings about even the most insignificant experiences. But even when we are not certain of what we are feeling, our emotions still have the power to dictate our actions. They act as a guide and a stimulus for response. To a degree, we have control over our feelings—we can either express or repress them. How we do this says much about our mental health.

We generally survive our feelings no matter how they are expressed, but we must live with the consequences. We can leave a situation with a positive afterglow or we can leave a swath of destruction. We can be delicate and diplomatic and hold our emotions in check or we can give them free rein with a no-holds-barred philosophy.

Intelligence and sensitivity remain our best guides. Feelings are essential to life and their appropriate expression is the balance to sustain it.

Emotion has taught mankind to reason.
MARQUIS DE VAUVENARGUES

The life and love
we create is the life
and love we live.

To love, we need not agree

Though it is essential for our well being that we please others, this must never be our prime purpose. It is impossible for anyone to please everyone all of the time. Still, trying to do so can become an obsession in which we begin to measure our worth in terms of how many people approve of us.

It is only when we have enough respect for our own uniqueness that we assert ourselves without the fear of rejection. Part of our uniqueness is our diversity of opinions, our own way of looking at the world. If we encounter those who do not accept this, all is not lost. It is possible for mature adults to disagree completely and still love. In fact, a loving relationship need not be an agreeing one. Disagreement can actually enhance a relationship. In the long run, when we stand up for who and what we are, we earn respect—from others and from ourselves.

Prejudgments become prejudices only if they are not reversible
when exposed to new knowledge.
GEORGE BANCROFT

The weight of guilt

If you have been carrying around an excessive burden of guilt, I have a simple suggestion: write the words, "I forgive me," on a piece of paper. Say these words over and over and over again. Don't stop until you get the message. Then throw it away, burn it, flush it—anything to be rid of it.

We spend so much time and energy browbeating ourselves over past mistakes. It's a wonder some of us can even move under such a weight of guilt.

The time has come to say, "enough!" If it is forgiveness we need, and it is not forthcoming, then we must ask for it, pleading our own ignorance if we must. We have a right to ask for understanding as well, because we are simply human, imperfect in so many ways. We must learn not to be controlled by guilt, while also learning to forgive those who inflict it upon us.

Without forgiveness life is governed by . . .
an endless cycle of resentment and retaliation.
ROBERT ASSAGIOLI

The value of our dreams

Hold on to your dreams for they are, in a sense, the stuff of which reality is made. It is through our dreams that we maintain the possibility of a better, more meaningful life. Even when reality imposes limits, our dreams continue to offer us a parade of opportunities.

Life has a way of becoming pretty mundane, even oppressively dull, if we succumb to it as it happens. But if we continue to enhance it with dreams, they can keep us stimulated and hopeful and striving.

I have had a million dreams. I dreamed of becoming a teacher, which, of course, meant years of expensive education. We were very poor and though neither Mama nor Papa ever discouraged me, they also did not encourage false hopes. Their dreams for me were more realistic, but I was determined to follow mine.

I had wild dreams of adventures in exotic lands, exploits of daring, scaling mountains, forging seas, canoeing rivers. Though I was assured that such a life was only for the special few, I refused to accept it as impossible for me. I am happy to report to all the skeptics around, that every dream I have ever had, I have made reality.

And I create new dreams every day.

It has been written that we are no greater than our dreams.
Dreams are the touchstones of our characters.
HENRY DAVID THOREAU

A healthy love of self

What we do not have, we cannot give. To love another, we must first have love ourselves. Still, there persists the idea that to love oneself is an egocentric, infantile, destructive notion. It was given passionate expression in the "psychedelic" Sixties and has since remained suspect as a sound concept.

Still simple logic tells us that we can only give what we possess and that the more we possess, the greater our capacity to give. If we truly love someone, it follows that we want them to have the best we have to offer, for their sake as well as ours. It is through an understanding and acceptance of ourselves, our needs and what we require for happiness that we can comprehend and appreciate the needs of others. Love has acquired its tenuous reputation because it has been, for so long, left in the hands of amateurs who distrust it and themselves.

Every single ancient wisdom and religion will tell
you the same thing—don't live entirely for yourself, live for
other people. Don't get stuck inside your own ego,
because it will become a prison in no time flat.
BARBARA WARD

Tears

Only those who have spent their lives totally preoccupied with themselves have never cried.

Tears are a form of compassionate thoughtfulness. They may be a visible sign that we've taken the focus from ourselves, however briefly, to feel with someone else. Each time we cry, we emerge with clearer eyes, cleaner vision. We become more able to identify and empathize with others and the human condition.

Only recently has our culture eased up its unwritten taboo against men crying. Traditionally, men were expected to display granite faces to the world. It was part of what defined them as "real men," unmoved, unflinching and emotionally straitjacketed. John Wayne and Gary Cooper, for instance, were not permitted to cry on screen, no matter what, until their later years when weakness and sentimentality could be explained as getting older.

A good healthy cry can be a sign of maturity. We've got it all wrong if we still believe that crying is a sign of weakness. Real weakness is in not allowing ourselves access to the emotions expressed through tears.

The greatest happiness you can have is knowing
that you do not necessarily require happiness.
WILLIAM SAROYAN

A *union of lovers*

We enrich the universe with something far more valuable than money when we contribute love. One act of caring may have more effect, more power than we can realize; here finding entry into a lonely heart, there encouraging and giving hope to a confused mind. The universal love story is written line by line with simple acts of loving people doing a kindness for someone who's having a hard time.

When we are truly loving, we become a part of a growing union of lovers whose strength comes from gentleness and whose example is in the selfless treatment of others. When we become active in this special union, we are forever enhancing and we are never alone.

One more good man on earth is better
than an extra angel in heaven.
CHINESE PROVERB

Love as the greatest possession

Many are convinced that possessions will make a difference and that they are measured by how much they possess. We exert great energies in collecting things until there is no more room in our homes, garages or offices for all the tokens of our experiences. It is not long before we realize that problems accumulate right along with our possessions. We need lawyers, financial planners, accountants to help us structure our lives. We must construct stronger safeguards to secure ourselves and our possessions. Peace of mind is purchased with louder alarms, greater police protection and insurance policies.

Without question, our society reinforces the idea of having more and then worshiping what we have. We are induced to buy and buy again, then discard and buy newer and better and more. It seems we are only reminded of the true value of love or life when we are faced with its loss. This is a lesson that is as old as human history and it still takes some of us a lifetime to learn it.

Happiness is inward, and not outward; and so,
it does not depend on what we have, but on what we are.
HENRY VAN DYKE

When it comes
to giving love, the
opportunities are
unlimited, and we
are all gifted.

The role of the past

We are a product of all the experiences we have known, all the people we have met, all the dreams we have or have not realized. We must always keep in mind, too, that people we love are a product of their yesterdays. They bring to us their fears, prejudices, triumphs, joys, all of which make them who they are at this point in time.

There is no denying our past, but neither should we be enslaved by it. It is ours to do with as we please. It has power over us only to the extent that it gives us some predictability for tomorrow. Living in the past is a sad alternative to living in the present.

Every relationship we form has the potential of enriching our present and enhancing our future. In the uniting of two or more special worlds, we bring together a combination of ideas, experiences and possibilities that have never been, nor will ever be again. This represents one of love's greatest joys and most subtle challenges.

We have limitless control over what might be.
ANONYMOUS

No one will think you worthy until you do

Self-esteem, though a much abused phrase, is basic to love and well being. Unless we feel worthy of love, we are not likely to receive it. The judgments we pass on ourselves are reflected in our every decision, our every act. If we care little for ourselves, we are likely to end up as someone's doormat.

Self-respect is the companion of self-worth. We can view the world as populated by individuals wiser, better looking, more interesting and desirable than we, or we can decide that we are just as valuable as they, only different. Instead of constantly comparing, we can focus on our unique strengths and use our energy to uncover dormant skills and new talents.

It is well to challenge ourselves with dreams of what we would like to be, but it is wiser to stay within the realistic realm of who we are. What wonders we do for our self-esteem when we accept who we are and look to our strengths rather than our weaknesses. When we accept ourselves, body mind and spirit, we will stop belittling ourselves and concentrate on the development of our potential for being the perfect us. At this point, we start to know what it means to be worthy of love.

Pride has a greater share than goodness of heart in the remonstrances we make to those who are guilty of faults; we reprove not so much with a view to correct them as to persuade them that we are exempt from those faults ourselves.
LA ROCHEFOUCAULD

Creating your own paradise

What do we expect from life and love, anyway? Few of us will discover a new continent, take a rocket to Jupiter, change history or become legendary lovers. Our life and our death will be of no momentous import, except to ourselves and those we love. Our days will probably be spent in eating, sleeping, working, washing clothes, growing gardens, raising children, getting sick and getting well, making new friends and saying good-bye to old ones, dressing in the morning and undressing at night, brushing our teeth and combing our hair, saving money and spending it, crying, laughing, getting angry and frustrated, finding moments of happiness and beauty, growing up, growing fat, growing old, dying.

If there is to be any poetry, romance, or meaning, it will be because we created it ourselves. The life and love we create is the life and love we live.

There is time for work. And there is time for love.
That leaves no other time.
COCO CHANEL

The blurred boundaries of intimacy

We are all in need of intimacy. We can love many people in varying degrees and in myriad ways, but we will always remain in need of one special relationship. We need someone with whom we feel a unique association, who gives us an essential feeling of security and comfort, as well as a degree of privacy, and deep affection that separates them from others. Generally there is a sexual dimension that in itself creates exclusivity. It is a physical and emotional bonding that brings strength and heals us in mysterious ways.

When love is accompanied with deep intimacy, it raises us to the highest level of human experience. In this exalted space, we can surrender our egos, become vulnerable and know levels of joy and well-being unique among life experiences. We attain a glimpse of the rapture that can be ours. Boundaries are blurred, there are no limitations and we rejoice in union. We become one and, at the same time, both.

There is only one happiness in life: to love and be loved.
GEORGE SAND

The value of loving

So many of us take life and love for granted, and bemoan the fact that we have so little control over either of them. We seldom slow down enough to consider the wonder of our existence and rarely take the time to appreciate its many miracles. We trash the world as if there were no limits to it and only occasionally consider our responsibility toward enhancing it.

Yet, the world is a generous place, giving so much and asking for so little. Every person on earth is a unique creation and is ours to discover and profit from. I am convinced that when we die, as we all must, we will not be held accountable for anything as much as how we valued our existence.

Creation, whether seen or unseen, must be, even now, about us
everywhere in the prosaic world of the present.
LOREN EISLEY

Escaping ourselves

Some of us believe we can rid ourselves of all of our troubles if only we could move our place of residence, surround ourselves with new people, change our job or go on a holiday. We forget that wherever we go, we take ourselves along. There is no escape from who we are. If we are depressed in Chicago, we'll be depressed in Spokane. If we feel lonely and alienated in San Francisco, we will also feel so in Atlanta, or Cairo, or Minden, or Miami.

When we do change our scenery, it may, for a time, make things seem better. Eventually, however, we are faced with the same alternatives to behavior, or lack thereof, the same attitudes, the same feelings. This is also true when seeking new lovers. We decide we have made a bad choice, so we stop the music and change partners. *Voila!* We're happy again for a time. But we bring into each new relationship our problems, our fears, our limitations. Soon we find ourselves back where we started, anxious, unhappy and looking for more.

It is so simple these days to end a relationship that there appears to be little motivation to even attempt to work at it. It seems easier to just move on down the road and try our luck again. If we are truly seeking the long-lasting love we all say we are, with the commitment, the satisfaction, and deep joy, there is only one way to achieve it. Changes will have to be made within instead of without. There is no other way.

We do have choice, but not without some agony.
JOSEPHINE HART

Love quiz

Asking yourself questions and answering them honestly is a good path to self-knowledge. In keeping with this idea, I'd like to propose a few end-of-the-day questions for each of us . . .

- Is anyone a little happier because I came along today?
- Did I leave any concrete evidence of my kindness, any sign of my love?
- Did I try to think of someone I know in a more positive light?
- Did I help someone to feel joy, to laugh, or at least, to smile?
- Have I attempted to remove a little of the rust that is corroding my relationships?
- Have I gone through the day without fretting over what I don't have and celebrating the things I do have?
- Have I forgiven others for being less than perfect?
- Have I forgiven myself?
- Have I learned something new about life, living or love?

If you are not satisfied with your answers, take heart. Tomorrow you get to start all over again! If you will it, this is one quiz you can never fail.

. . . if I am to be entitled to my happiness,
I must not only earn it for myself, but dispense it.
RALPH BARTON PERRY

Aging love?

Whenever I am privileged to speak with a group of elderly people, I have an insatiable desire for them to share their memories, their philosophies. It is sad that the experiences and thoughts of the aging in our country are so often relegated to reminiscences of the good old days. So much wisdom from so many valuable years of experience is being lost because of our callous and unthinking attitude that human worth diminishes as we grow older.

It is not surprising to me that the topic of love is a dominant one among our older population. It is a subject that always recalls common and vivid experiences. And so it should be since love is the centerpiece and the one common thread in each of our lives from cradle to grave.

Something that a lovely, wise 81-year-old woman shared at a seminar once has stayed with me over the years. In being asked what her needs were in this latter stage of life, she said very simply, "All I need and ever needed was someone to love and someone to love me. Nothing's changed."

God must have realized humans need to be
connected with the past, so he gave us memories.
MIKE RUHLAND

Any action that inhibits is not love. Love is only love when it liberates.

The miracle of love

Sometimes it is difficult to remember, but it remains nonetheless true, that not too long ago we were all children. For most children, faith is unwavering. Joy is a natural state. They seldom worry. They laugh and play a lot. They live in a world of wondrous anticipation where miracles are commonplace.

Actually, nothing has really changed now that we have become adults except our attitudes and the way we choose to see things. The wonder, the mystery, the magic, the sources of amusement are all still there if we look.

Miracles can occur anywhere. When someone cares, when years of animosity and resentment disappear in one act of compassion, when indifference is wiped away by an outstretched hand offered to help, when a human life is changed by one simple act of love—these are indeed miracles.

In a world where pessimism and cynicism are valued, "anything is possible" has such a refreshing, hopeful sound to it.

The next time you need a miracle, don't wait for it to happen. You have the power to create it.

It is man's destiny to ponder on the riddle
of existence and, as a by-product of his wonderment,
to create a new life on this earth.
CHARLES F. KETTERING

Love doesn't have forever

Anyone who has ever read much of what I have written over the years recognizes the above as a familiar theme. It is a subject that I have admittedly belabored, but with reason. I have found that most of us tend to get so wrapped up in the trivialities of living, that we forget to live. Today is the time for doing, for going places, for giving happiness, for accomplishing the things we've relegated to the land of "some day, when the time is right."

We don't need to think of each day as potentially our last. This would be as frantically nonproductive as putting things off, but by the same token, we must resist with determination that dull complacency which lulls us into the belief that we always have tomorrow.

Today well-lived makes every yesterday a dream of happiness,
and every tomorrow a vision of hope.
SALUTATION TO THE DAWN

How about?
An afterword . . . .

How about?

Once when I was in Denver I found I desperately needed a post office. The directions I was given led me everywhere but the post office. After touring half of downtown, I finally questioned a hotel doorman. He recognized me. "What are you doing in Denver?" he asked.

"I'm doing a lecture here," I answered.

"Really!' he exclaimed with enthusiasm. "What are you gonna talk about?"

"Finding Your Way To Love," I told him.

"That's a riot!" he laughed. "You're gonna be telling all those people how to find love and you can't even find your way to the post office!"

As I indicated in the preface of this book, I am in no way an expert in anything, not on love and least of all not on how to find your way to a post office in a strange city. But this book was never intended as a "how to." What I have attempted to do is focus our thoughts on love and create a space in which we might more readily study it; the pattern, processes and changes essential for its realization and enhancement.

Love makes for exhilarating study, for only in the act of loving are we sufficiently distracted from ourselves to view, even momentarily, a glimpse of our true selves. We need not fear this. We can only profit from the disclosure if we do not fall prey to the very human temptation of going back to antiquated, useless, destructive habits, beliefs, and behaviors.

Love offers us the most unabashedly sumptuous experience of which we are humanly capable. It awaits only a decision on our part to act. Do so and a world of love is yours!

We are, indeed, born for love.

Index of Quotations